Cuban Color in Tourism
and *La Lucha*

ISSUES OF GLOBALIZATION
Case Studies in Contemporary
Anthropology

*Labor and Legality: An Ethnography of a Mexican
Immigrant Network*
Ruth Gomberg-Muñoz

*"Walking Together in the Forest": An Ethnography of
Foraging and Farming Women of the Congo Basin*
Bonnie Hewlett

Cuban Color in Tourism and La Lucha: *An
Ethnography of Racial Meanings*
L. Kaifa Roland

Cuban Color in Tourism and *La Lucha*

An Ethnography of Racial Meanings

L. Kaifa Roland
University of Colorado at Boulder

New York   Oxford
OXFORD UNIVERSITY PRESS
2011

Oxford University Press, Inc., publishes works that further Oxford University's
objective of excellence in research, scholarship, and education.

Oxford   New York
Auckland   Cape Town   Dar es Salaam   Hong Kong   Karachi
Kuala Lumpur   Madrid   Melbourne   Mexico City   Nairobi
New Delhi   Shanghai   Taipei   Toronto

With offices in
Argentina   Austria   Brazil   Chile   Czech Republic   France   Greece
Guatemala   Hungary   Italy   Japan   Poland   Portugal   Singapore
South Korea   Switzerland   Thailand   Turkey   Ukraine   Vietnam

Copyright © 2011 by Oxford University Press, Inc.

Published by Oxford University Press, Inc.
198 Madison Avenue, New York, New York 10016
http://www.oup.com

Oxford is a registered trademark of Oxford University Press

Library of Congress Cataloging-in-Publication Data

Roland, L. Kaifa (Lorecia Kaifa)
    Cuban color in tourism and la lucha : an ethnography of racial meanings / L. Kaifa Roland.
        p. cm.
    Includes bibliographical references and index.
    ISBN 978-0-19-973966-0
1. Tourism—Cuba. 2. Culture and tourism—Cuba. 3. Culture and globalization—Cuba.
4. Cuba—Race relations. 5. Cuba—Social life and customs.   I. Title.
    G155.C9R65 2010
    972.9106'4—dc22   2010007438

Printed in the United States of America
on acid-free paper

To my daughter, Asha:

Con la esperanza de que la Cuba que llegues a conocer en tu vida sea libre—en todos los sentidos.

CONTENTS

PREFACE

I like to think of ethnography as "a portrait of a people" that captures broad cultural patterns from the finest details of daily life. The problem that ethnographers encounter is that the subject usually must sit still for the portrait! Especially since the fall of the Soviet Union in 1989, Cuba has been in a state of rapid change that casts the ethnographer's findings into the realm of history before they have been fully analyzed. The rise of tourism as the engine of Cuba's socialist economy has profound implications for the Cuban revolution, for Cuban culture more broadly, and for other sites of international tourism. Special Period Cuba teaches enduring lessons about belonging in the contexts of race, nation, and tourism.

To highlight longstanding cultural patterns (as well as newer ones), this book requires a broad historical context that dates from before Cuba's independence at the dawn of the twentieth century. *Cuban Color* centrally asks what "belonging" means in a nationalist context, and how that meaning translates in the context of mass international tourism. In other words, I use tourism as a lens to bring Cuban culture into clearer focus. I find that the issues of race, gender, and international class highlighted by contemporary tourism in Cuba are not creations of the post-Soviet present but are foundational to Cuban identity regardless of time or place.

Implications of the Study

These issues also have implications in a variety of wide-ranging contexts. First, the focus on tourism has relevance to any number of developing countries that rely on tourism as the center of their economy. Certainly, each country has its own specific historical context (which deserve more attention than this book can provide), but the issues of status and belonging for tourists and their hosts are replicated in many sites. Whereas Cuba's socialist ideology features in the desire to maintain separate spheres for Cubans and tourists, in East African sites of cultural tourism, for example, the desire to maintain the illusion of indigeneity motivates a similar segregation of tourists from their increasingly modern host population (see Bruner 2005). The racialization implicit in the Cuban case pushes us to think about whether the separate worlds in which tourists and hosts dwell should be considered inherently unequal.

This book also highlights the constructed nature of race and draws directly from Cuban understandings of color and status to argue for a racialized conception of tourists and Cubans that does not depend solely on skin color. While anthropologists have long posited race to be a cultural construct, we do not always clarify what this means in practice. Rather, we tend to continue to theorize as though blackness and whiteness are the sole determinants of "race." My repeated use of the more active terms "racialize" and "racialization," as well as the descriptive "racial," seeks to remind readers of the constructed nature of race. Skin color is only one aspect of Cuban racial understandings, which include performative (or behavioral) features that extend into tourism. This approach has particular relevance in places where ethnic distinctions predominate over racial ones like in tourism to Eastern Europe, Africa, or Asia.

Lastly, this research has relevance for understanding what nationalism means at the level of day-to-day practice. While states may posit a particular nationalist ideology—in Cuba's case, the state ideology is socialism—everyday life may not always mesh with that vision. It is necessary, therefore, to illustrate how people interact with ideology on the ground: do they buy into it, ignore it, talk back to it, or manipulate it? The Cuban case—filled with *luchadores*, *buscadores*, *bisneros*, and *jineteros*—demonstrates that they do all of these things and more.

A common thread that runs through literature on tourism, race, and nationalism is the need to distinguish between Us and Them, the Self and the Other. All speak to theories of belonging, to which I hope *Cuban Color* contributes while highlighting the need for future research on this pivotal concept.

Organization

Chapter 1 introduces the book's central arguments about the racialization that I perceive to be central to tourism as practiced in Cuba today, while considering tourism's capitalistic implications in the context of the socialist revolution. The chapter concludes with an explanation of my research methodology. Chapter 2 considers the question of Cuban identity, tracing Cuban conceptions of race and blackness historically from the prerevolutionary era through the contemporary Special Period (a timeline is included at the end of the book). It historically grounds the subsequent chapters in order to demonstrate parallels as well as divergences in the racialized tourist encounters I describe in the present. Chapter 3 is an ethnographic analysis of everyday life in the world of Cubans. It extends the racialized concept of *cultura* described in the previous chapter to the contemporary Special Period *lucha* (or struggle) to survive. It also considers the increased individualism and decline in state authority in Cuba's late-socialist context, showing how revolutionary ethics and propaganda are often at odds with what people must do to get by.

Chapter 4 incorporates foreign tourists into the Cuban landscape. Considering global power in terms of race, place, and gender, as well as what that power means for Cuba's revolutionary project, the chapter extends arguments made in the third chapter about the growing racial implications of privilege, power, and belonging that resonate in sites of Cuban–tourist interaction. Chapter 5 concludes the book by revisiting the generational significance of the revolution with an eye toward the contemporary importance of capitalist tools in Cuba's socialist system. The epilogue updates some of the ethnographic data in light of follow-up visits in July 2007 and July 2008 during the transition from Fidel Castro's long period of leadership to the rise of his brother, Raul. Changes in street terminology reveal a hardened *lucha* context amid the continued racialization of Cubans and tourists.

Audience

Cuban Color is written with two primary audiences in mind: (1) undergraduate students in introductory or advanced courses on Cuba, the Caribbean, tourism, race, or cultural anthropology, and (2) fellow scholars who seek a novel approach either to Cuba or to the ethnographic endeavor. In addition to glossaries in English and Spanish, there is a Student Resource Guide to support classroom use that contains chapter-specific exercises, and additional (film and online) resources located at the end of the book.

In addition to these primary audiences, I hope this book enlightens everyday Americans about Cuban realities so they may engage knowledgeably in broader policy discussions. And, most importantly, I hope the many Cubans who contributed to this book recognize their experiences and culture to be truthfully represented.

Acknowledgments

If I learned nothing else from my experiences in Cuba, I learned the importance of social relationships, so I am grateful for the opportunity to thank the many individuals and entities that made the research for *Cuban Color* possible. First, I thank my parents for the example they set for my sisters and me to always press toward our intellectual limits. In a world that told us it was not "cool" for black youths to study, they succeeded in raising three young women who all hold postgraduate degrees, as does each of them.

Next, I thank the Duke University Cultural Anthropology Department, first for giving me a chance in the doctoral program, but more for the intellectual stimulation provided while I was there. Special thanks go to my advisor, mentor, and friend, Deborah Thomas (now at the University of Pennsylvania), who worked closely with me in earlier stages of this project.

In the later stages, my sister-friends—Carla Jones, Carole McGranahan, and Donna Goldstein—from the University of Colorado Anthropology Department writing group have been of invaluable assistance not only with the book but also in my development as a professional anthropologist. Thanks also go to Bianca Williams in Ethnic Studies for her advice and friendship, as well as to Dennis McGilvray in Anthropology for his mentorship.

Jan Beatty, Cory Schneider, and the reviewers for Oxford University Press helped me turn a manuscript into a book. Those reviewers include: Connie M. Anderson, Hartwick College; Sharon A. Carstens, Portland State University; Gina Hunter, Illinois State University; Laura Lewis, James Madison University; Kathe Managan, Louisiana State University; Rachel Newcomb, Rollins College; Phyllis Passariello, Centre College; and, Miriam Shakow, Vanderbilt University. Special thanks go to Nancy Mann, who provided extensive copyediting assistance.

There are many more thanks to go around, especially since I was unable to obtain outside funding to conduct dissertation research in "the forbidden land of Cuba." My Duke graduate stipend as well as awards and fellowships granted by Duke's Graduate School, the Center for International Studies, and the Atlantic Working Group of Oceans Connect funded my research and travel costs. Friends and family also sent money (or hired me) to help me financially, as well as their prayers to sustain me spiritually. Kim Sims provided invaluable support by taking care of my daughter while I made final revisions. While I cannot name everyone, special thanks go to my sisters, Leslie and Lisa, for always being there.

While my research funding was something of a patchwork affair, I was able to write the dissertation on which *Cuban Color* is based without any financial worries thanks to the Kenyon College Minority Dissertation Fellowship. I am grateful to the Anthropology and Sociology Departments, as well as the African American Faculty Caucus, for welcoming me as a colleague and a friend. I also appreciate my students from Kenyon, Duke, and the University of Colorado who have challenged and inspired me.

My concluding thanks go to my friends and family in Cuba: *He tratado de protegérles no usando sus nombres verdaderos, pero Uds. saben quienes son. Gracias a todos por su ayuda. Especialmente a mi familia, yo no hubiese podido sobrevivir por un día en Cuba sin las lecciones que me dieron sobre su país y la vida.*

While I share with all of you any accolades this book may receive, I accept any shortcomings as mine alone.

CHAPTER 1

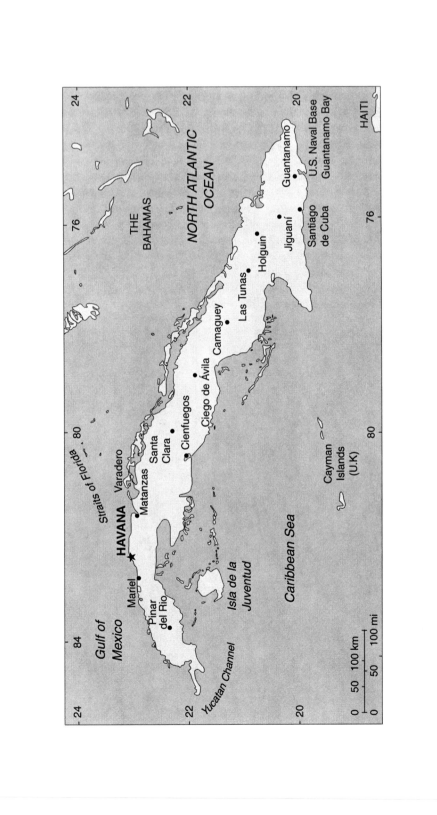

Race, Tourism, and Belonging in Cuba

Two days after arriving in Cuba for the very first time in 1999, I joined a group of students on my study tour to indulge in Havana's much acclaimed nightlife. Within a few steps of leaving our hotel on the El Prado boulevard, two young men from the group were approached by a couple of *jineteros*—street hustlers. The hustlers led us to a bar in Central Havana's Chinatown. Once there, our group of twelve all opted to order *mojitos*—the tourist "welcome" drink of fresh mint and sugar, ground with a pestle and mixed with rum, seltzer water, and ice. As people got their drinks, everyone commented on how delicious they were. But when I finally tasted my *mojito*—the last one served—I wondered at the praise I had been hearing: mine tasted like seltzer water with a little mint in it. I tasted a few other people's drinks and realized that only my drink had been watered down in this way. I sent the drink back twice, but it remained unacceptable.

By now furious, I realized that this was a racial situation, for I was the only African American member traveling with this group of white American students. We were all dressed in casual summer attire; only my race distinguished me from my colleagues. My preliminary reading had led me to understand that racism was practiced rather subtly in Latin America's "racial democracies." Yet even growing up in the U.S. South, I had never before been made to feel my skin color so poignantly. When I was eventually introduced to the *jineteros*, who had, by then, attached themselves to our group, their embarrassment was visible. "Oh my goodness," one of them exclaimed as the other disappeared, "we thought you were Cuban!" I asked if that was why my drink was unpalatable. Ashamedly, he nodded yes. When I asked why, he told me that since I had appeared to tag along toward the back of the group, and most of all because of my skin color, they assumed I was a *prostituta*.[1] From that point on, I always placed myself in the center of whatever group I was with, but it made no differ-ence. If we walked into a hotel nightclub, the security guards would let the others pass without incident but step directly in my path, asking me where I was going. I quickly learned to look confused and to respond in my best American-accented English that I did not understand because I did not speak Spanish. Only on very few occasions, in encounters with the police, did I have to prove my foreigner status by showing the photocopy of my passport that I had learned to keep with me at all times.

Welcome to Cuba

Over the course of my field research in Cuba from 1999 to 2003, I would hear time and again how "Cuban" I looked or how "Cubanized" my actions had become. While I was there, I seldom theorized much about such exchanges, given that even at home in the United States people fre-quently attributed my dark complexion and my dreadlocked hairstyle to a Caribbean heritage. It was only when I returned from the field and began to think about the data I had collected in light of my initial research question—"How has contemporary tourism changed Cuban culture and society?"—that I began to recognize what it meant to be (or to be mis-taken for) Cuban in the context of Cuba's increasing reliance on tourism as a means to sustain its **socialist system**. It became clear to me as a black female foreigner (see Simmons 2001) that Cuban identity was being racial-ized—blackened, if you will—vis-à-vis the (white) foreign Other in a way that conformed to traditional, prerevolutionary Cuban understandings of race (see Roland 2006).

Although racial understandings have played a significant role in shap-ing Cuban social relations through the present, race tends to be written out of analyses of Cuba's past and present politico-economic processes because of the prerevolutionary policy of "whitening" and the revolu-tionary belief that removing class exploitation would also eradicate racial discrimination. As the next chapter shows more extensively, whitening or **blanqueamiento** is the attempt in many Latin American societies to eliminate evidence of an African presence both physically (by such means as miscegenation and importation of Europeans) and culturally (by elimi-nating "Africanisms" in such areas as religion, music, and dance). Further, just as Brazilians affirm an imagined **racial democracy**, Cubans celebrate their **mestizo** or mixed heritage and consider **discourse** that posits racial discrimination to be unpatriotic (McGarrity and Cárdenas 1995; Twine 1998; Wade 1993; Wright 1990).[2] In recent scholarship, blacks are gen-erally perceived to be among the greatest beneficiaries of the revolution, especially given Fidel Castro's proclamations that Cubans are an "Afro-Latin" people (de la Fuente 2001; C. Moore 1988; Sawyer 2006); indeed, I found that the general populace seems to accept that *el color no importa*—color doesn't matter—despite realities of racial discrimination and prejudice in day-to-day practice (see Roland 2004 and Twine 1998).

This book analyzes interactions between Cubans and tourists in order to consider how **global capitalism** articulates at the local level in today's socialist Cuba. Drawing from my **ethnographic** research among both Cubans and foreign tourists at the dawn of the twenty-first century, I argue that in day-to-day practice, the same tourism that props up the socialist system also significantly challenges the system's ideology by reasserting prerevolutionary meanings of race and class on a **transnational**, yet intrapersonal plane. Specifically, international tourism racializes not only individual Cubans and foreign tourists, but also their countries of origin. That is, if Europe and Canada—as well as the many other countries from which tourists come—are understood to be white (as is demonstrated through the use of the colloquial term *yuma*, discussed extensively in the course of the book), Cubans perceive themselves to be onerously black by comparison (see Yelvington 2001).[3]

This book explores the tensions and contradictions of post-Soviet-era Cuba's use of tourism, a fundamentally capitalist tool, to sustain its socialist economy. Since the revolution took on its socialist character in 1961, Cuba's political and intellectual leaders have fostered a national identity characterized by raceless and classless egalitarianism through such institutions as the educational system and the workplace. A "New Man's" work ethic has been promoted, one that privileges moral over material incentives, and a pride in Cuba for Cubans (Guevara 1965; see also Serra 2007). However, the Cuban government's response to changes in the global economy after the 1989 fall of the Soviet Union—opening to a peso-dollar dual economy and promoting entrepreneurship, foreign investment, and tourism—has engendered a culture of survival that often undermines these revolutionary aspirations. Specifically, an emergent racialization is being revived within the space created by the vast economic gap between foreign tourists and their Cuban hosts.

Given developing countries' increasing reliance on mass international tourism, this argument has relevance in places as near to Cuba as the Bahamas and as far away as Thailand (see Dupuy 2001 and Clarke and Thomas 2006). Certainly, each locale has its own unique history and differentiated understandings of raciality (Harrison 1995; Holt 2000; Yelvington 2001), but I propose that one of the consequences of importing large numbers of wealthy foreigners to tour previously colonized lands is a reinvigoration of notions of entitlement: Who is allowed where, and what are the entitled people supposed to be doing in those spaces? Under what circumstances are boundaries between tourists and Cubans crossed? What are the consequences of being where one does not belong, and who enforces the dividing lines? Such questions from the colonial period are replicated in the touristic context but further complicated by a new nationalist impetus that seeks full independence (see Sørensen 1997). In both historical moments, a (largely) white minority group is wealthy and privileged in comparison to a (largely) black or brown majority of working people who are outsiders to the sites of leisure and power.

The Meaning(s) of "Race"

In July 2008, I had been drinking a few Mayabe beers at a music festival on Havana's five-mile-long sea wall known as the Malecón with Pipo, a Michael Jordan lookalike, when I (again) needed a restroom. Opting to exercise my tourist persona, I refused to use the indescribably filthy port-a-john I had used some twenty minutes earlier. Before I could explain my intention to go to the popular Fiat fast-food restaurant a few blocks away, Pipo led me toward the top-tier Pato Ciego tourist nightclub across the plaza. I happily went along, figuring he knew better than I.

When we arrived, Pipo explained my urgent need to the large black male bouncer posted at the door. The man shook his head and said the ladies' room was being repaired before the evening show in a few hours. Changing tactics, Pipo explained that I was a guest from the United States; perhaps I could use the men's room instead? The man apologized and watched us hurry down the steps as Pipo decided where we should go next. He located a lower-scale tourist club a few blocks up the Vedado neighborhood's steep *la Rampa* incline. This time he decided to pretend he was American too. The *mestiza* woman who stood outside Restaurante Monsieur displaying a menu to prospective patrons immediately intercepted us. To Pipo's explanation in (what he thought was) Anglicized Spanish that we wanted to dine, she responded that we could not enter because I was wearing flip-flops. After his performed translation, I explained in English that we had just been in the hotel pool and were hungry. Not understanding, she confirmed with Pipo that I did not know any Spanish; only then did she let us sit at an inconspicuous table. I asked where the restroom was and she pointed to it; then, as she handed Pipo the menu, I heard her tell him, "Please don't talk too loudly because of the light piano music." I nearly stumbled in my tracks when I, with my black American ear, translated her to have said, "Don't be in here acting like *negros de la calle* [blacks off the street]." When I returned from the restroom (having passed three white tourists in flip-flops at their more centrally located tables), Pipo confirmed what she had said. As we left the restaurant without having ordered, we smiled and thanked the young woman for her help. On our way back to the Malecón we considered our different reactions to her words. He had perceived nothing problematic about her assumption that we—two dark-complexioned black people—might "talk too loudly" until I brought it to his attention.

Anthropology and Race

Anthropologists have been theorizing the meanings of race since the founding of the discipline in the late 1800s (Baker 1998). Certainly skin color had accrued meaning before this time, especially given Europe's global colonial expansion from the 1500s; however, the late-eighteenth-century Age of Reason fostered among Europe's ruling elite a newfound interest in scientific explanation as opposed to religious or superstition-based explanations. Race became a particularly salient topic of scientific analysis in the Americas because of the increasingly fixed links between social status and color among the indigenous, European, African, and later Asian people inhabiting the New World. The earliest anthropological analyses played a central role in creating the racial categories and meanings that today's anthropologists seek to deconstruct (see Trouillot 1991).

Specifically, **social Darwinist** Herbert Spencer (1820–1923) grafted Charles Darwin's laws of natural selection onto human societies, proposing that in the "Survival of the Fittest" the lighter races were superior to the darker races. This **essentialist** viewpoint perceived the races as fixed in their capacities; the distinctions between them should not (and could not) be altered. Social Darwinists believed the races should remain separate and certainly should not interbreed (Baker 1998; Stocking 1994). By contrast, **cultural evolutionists** like Lewis Henry Morgan (1818–1881) suggested that the inferior status of the darker races was not permanent; instead he linked each race's cultural level to its material conditions. This perspective presumes that culture is hierarchical, with hunter-gatherer societies less "developed" or of lower culture than agricultural ones, which in turn were less developed than industrial ones. Numerous training schools for Native Americans and postemancipation African Americans sought to prove that it was possible to make the world's darker-skinned people culturally "white" (see Baker 1998). In other words, cultural evolutionists perceived racial characteristics in terms of a continuum of physical and cultural progress that was inherited but adaptable depending on the environment (Baker 1998; Stocking 1994). As the next chapter explains more extensively, the ruling classes in Cuba and other racially intermixed societies in Latin America tended toward the cultural evolutionist perspective on race, whereas the ruling classes in the British colonies generally preferred the social Darwinist approach.

As the "Father of American Anthropology," Franz Boas (1858–1942) was central in shifting the long-standing hierarchical conception of race to the more relativistic approach increasingly accepted among many North Americans, which envisioned "races" in relation to multiple cultures rather than a single hierarchically ranked Culture. Boas and the **cultural relativists** argued that the meanings signified by skin color or "race" are **culturally constructed**; that is, each cultural group assigns meanings to physical differences (including bone structure, eye shape, nose shape, hair texture, lip size, skin color) depending on its own historical context. Those meanings, then, are based not in nature, but rather in culture (see Benedict 1940 and Montagu 1942). Nonetheless, constructed or not, culturally assigned racial meanings still resonate in people's lives (Omi and Winant 1986).

Like other constructs such as gender, sexuality, and status (whether class or national), "race" often operates on a naturalized and therefore invisible plane. In U.S. society, for example, "race" is often used in reference to "blacks" or other minority groups, and gender is generally used to refer to "women" or "females"; whiteness is not seen as raced, nor maleness as gendered. Even in this book, which seeks to highlight Cuban constructions of race in order to suggest their relationship to the contemporary Cuban tourism industry, the reader may occasionally get the sense that "race" disappears. Perhaps this is to be expected given that Cuba's national doctrine deemphasizes skin color as a determinant of belonging. As Pipo's and my experience reveals, even (or especially) Cubans of African descent have been socialized to maintain Cuba's myth of racial democracy by "turning down the volume" on racial messages, whereas African Americans "hear" race at a higher intensity given the United States' history of **Jim Crow** segregation laws, Civil Rights activism, and Black Power ideology. In other words, even when unspoken, as in my restroom adventure, culturally specific meanings of blackness, *mulato*-ness, and whiteness remain in operation.

Racial Constructions in the Americas

As the scholars cited previously have demonstrated, the culturally specific assumptions about whiteness and blackness that are taken for granted in the United States often find their meanings lost or altered in other contexts. Throughout Latin America and the Caribbean, complex classifications of color are linked with expectations regarding education, social status, and value. While before the Civil Rights Movement in the United States some blacks might achieve middle-class status—even without "passing" as white—they still indisputably "belonged" among blacks. By contrast, in Latin American countries like Brazil, Colombia, Venezuela, and Cuba, individual blacks might rise to middle- (or even upper-) class status, but they were perceived by the broader society—both black and white—to be exceptional, and therefore "white" or otherwise "whitened" (e.g., *mulato*; Degler 1971). The point that Latin Americans were socialized to overlook in such cases of black social mobility was that *in general* blackness (and to a lesser extent mixed-ness) was associated with negative characteristics like poverty, stupidity, and unattractiveness, while whiteness signified wealth, intelligence, and beauty (Degler 1971).

The mixed race (*mulato* or **pardo**) category in Latin America shared many characteristics with the intermediate racial category of "browns" or "coloreds" in the British Caribbean. Whereas in either case this mixed-race group may have had access to occupations closed to blacks or *negros*, in the Anglo-Caribbean there remained a fixed social line dividing this group from whites. Similarly, while upwardly mobile blacks might enter the lower rungs of the mixed population in both the Latin and the Anglo American countries, only in Latin America and the French Caribbean could *mulatos* aspire to penetrate the white social and professional sphere. In any case, as Harry Hoetink (1985) reminds us, "the whole racial power structure conspires to encourage the colored elite to emulate the white groups both culturally and in physical appearance (fostering a desire for 'whitening' or 'improving the race')" (70).

Anthropologists working in the United States have recently begun to recognize how notions of "race" can come unhinged from a strict color basis, even in the context of a single racial group. Writing about inner-city Detroit's white communities, John Hartigan (1999) finds that whiteness—that is, acceptable whiteness—is dependent upon conformity to the white middle-class norms of education, income, "liberal" or progressive thought, and the distance those norms remove whites from blackness. In the Detroit context that he studies, "hillbillies'" social nearness to blackness makes their whiteness questionable, especially in the eyes of middle-class whites. Similarly, in his analysis of Harlem, New York, John L. Jackson (2001) finds education, occupation, and income to be defining features of a behaviorally based "blackness" that involves such areas as: "The way one wears one's hair, walks, talks, stands, makes passes, or wears one's clothes" (2001, 148).

Both Hartigan and Jackson define blackness and whiteness as contrasting identities—with whiteness signifying privilege and refinement, while blackness connotes hardship and base instinctiveness. There is a similar contrast in Cuba's racial context (see especially chapter 2 on "Raciality"). Moreover, both theorists find phenotypical color to be challenged by socially understood meanings of race as determined by in-group members who uphold the norm. In everyday practice, "race" is determined not only by skin color but also by the way one behaves (or is perceived to behave) in relation to the rest of the group. Again, a similar phenomenon is at work in the Cuban tourist industry.

Tourism and the Caribbean

I sat alone amid a crowd of some five hundred people—mostly Cubans—at the Vallecaballos Hotel in Cienfuegos on July 26, 2000—the forty-seventh anniversary of the ill-fated attack on the Moncada barracks in Santiago-de-Cuba by Fidel Castro and his cadre that is now a national holiday (called "*26 de julio*") marking the beginning of the Cuban revolution. People had stood solemnly in honor of the national anthem, but afterwards the Cuba Libre drinks of rum and cola began to flow. The theme of the show—filled with children's choirs and glitzy performances by professional dance troupes—was "Cuba as part of the Caribbean."

Since Cuba has often identified itself, and been identified by others, less as a Caribbean nation than as a Latin American or even socialist one, I wondered whether the choice of this theme for a nationalist celebration had been affected by the fall of the Soviet Union and the subsequent increased reliance on tourism within the Cuban economy. Indeed, a significant finding of this study is that the post-Soviet **Special Period** has realigned Cuba with the Caribbean in terms of economic options and the effects of **globalization**, despite Cuba's different history and its having served as a model of anti-imperialism for Caribbean populations over the course of the revolution.

The Caribbean was colonized in the sixteenth and seventeenth centuries by the British, French, and Dutch as well as the Spanish, and with the advent of the transatlantic slave trade, it had a high ratio of enslaved African laborers to European settlers (Hoetink 1985; Mintz 1989). Thus the forces of globalization have always been central in the Caribbean. The distinct colonial regimes differentiated Caribbean cultural practices not only along linguistic lines, but also in terms of political and cultural nearness to the European **metropole** (Hoetink 1985; Knight 2005).

As many island nations of the Caribbean (and the Pacific) that had previously been sustained by monocrop plantation economies became politically independent of colonial relationships in the nineteenth and twentieth centuries, national leaders were forced to consider their available

resources to sustain the newly independent nations. Though the political and economic constraints of colonialism had begun to wane in the years following the World Wars, **international lending organizations**—like the World Bank and the International Monetary Fund (IMF)—used economic incentives to strongly encourage developing countries to industrialize and "modernize" their economies in ways that often linked them in a subordinate economic position to wealthier, "developed" nations of the modern West (Lewis 1985; see also Black 2001).

While many Caribbean islands had received some travelers and tourists from the United States or the colonial metropole before the 1940s, most reshaped their economies to focus on tourism only in the decades that followed. Spaces that had previously been imagined as mosquito-ridden hotbeds of disease were remade through creative marketing as sites of therapeutic rest and relaxation (Taylor 1993). Beginning in a country's cooler mountain areas and moving toward the coastal zones as European aversion to the sun subsided, island tourism grew incrementally. Palm trees and beaches soon became emblems of leisure in nature.

Seeking to exploit tourists' nostalgic sensibilities, leaders of these new tourist destinations often had to struggle mightily to convince the descendants of slaves that basing their economy on a service industry would ultimately benefit the new nation's quest for self-determination. Blacks working as cooks, housekeepers, waiters, and bellmen replicated the work of house-slaves of previous generations. Tourism marketing built on such racialized and gendered representations as the eroticized exotic Other—especially the woman of racially mixed ancestry. Known as *La Mulata* in Cuba (see chapter 2, "Gendered Race"), she was caricatured in advertising inviting tourists to visit her country and lose all the inhibitions of home (see Figure 1.1; Alexander 1997; Cohen 1995; Enloe 1990; Schwartz 1997).

In addition to jobs in the service industry, tourism promised jobs in such related areas as construction (hotels, roads), agriculture (produce for hotels), and textiles (souvenirs and tourist markets). As a "domestic export," it was anticipated that tourism would allow host countries to retain the economic gains provided by the industry. After some fifty years of practice, this promise of tourism has never been wholly fulfilled because of what are known as **leakages** (de Kadt 1979; Enloe 1990). Because the majority of developing countries cannot afford to build the tourism infrastructure on their own, corporations based in other countries provide those services. Most of the profits generated by a hotel (or restaurant or airline) then go to the transnational corporation rather than to the host country. Further, tourists often prefer familiar foods and toiletries from their home countries to "exotic" local products. While some local fruits

FIGURE **1.1**   1950s Ad – "Light-hearted Latin gayety...vivid foreign charm in nearby Cuba" (author's collection)

The text of the advertisement reads, "Share Cuba's famed hospitality...the foreign beauty of this musical and magical Isle! Here—only 90 miles from the U.S.—you'll find a dazzlingly *different* year-long sun-land combining a wealth of new diversions in a setting of leisurely Latin charm. Enjoy Havana's Continental pleasures—Carnival and fiestas, gaming, sports events. Visit centuries old cities...lovely beaches like Varadero... historic landmarks...renowned spas...the legendary Isle of Pines. You reach Cuba quickly, easily, inexpensively, by frequent air or sea transportation. You travel within Cuba by efficient, comfortable plane, bus or train. It's simple to bring your own car; over 700 miles of fine highway beckon. No passports needed for U.S. citizens. Average winter temperature 73°" (emphasis in original).

and produce are used in the tourism industry to remind tourists "where they are," there are also many leakages through the importation of expensive goods from abroad. In the end, the benefits of tourism have amounted mostly to the recuperation of taxes from transnational entities (now threatened by increasing **liberalization**; see "Post-socialist Globalization" later), and the provision of low-paying, low-skill jobs to large numbers of people in a host society (Brunt and Courtney 1999; de Kadt 1979).

The socialist revolution of 1959 largely interrupted mass international tourism to Cuba because most of its market had been from the United States. One of the rallying cries early in the revolution was "Cuba for Cubans" in protest of Cuban exclusion from tourist spaces. Moreover, socialism's new moral order conceived of tourism as bourgeois materialism—one means by which the wealthy classes exercised their domination over the working classes. Still, because Communism had yet to be perfected, vacations remained a necessary incentive for socialist workers. The small-scale tourism industry that remained in Cuba focused on the needs of the Soviet bloc, featuring high-ranking Russian and East German officials. **Vanguard** workers from Cuba and other members of the Soviet alliance also vacationed in sites of Cuban tourism during the hot off-season. On the whole, however, as Cubans went about "building the revolution" from the 1960s through the 1980s they also sought to dismantle the country's earlier "playground" reputation, replacing it with the image of Cuba as an example of anti-imperialism for other developing countries to emulate.

Socialism and Cuba's Revolutionary Ideal

Before the Special Period, every revolutionary speech ended with the predictable slogan that articulated the revolution's anti–U.S.-imperialist stance: "¡*Patria o Muerte! ¡¡Venceremos!!*" (Homeland or death! We will be victorious!!). When the Soviet Union began to open to the global economy under Mikhail Gorbachev's **perestroika** (restructuring) policy in the late 1980s, the Cuban government looked on with concern and hardened its resolve as the country's primary financial benefactor shifted their ideological strategy. By the time the Soviet Union had fallen and the Eastern bloc had been dismantled, Cuba had revised its slogan to *Socialismo o Muerte* (Socialism or Death), clearly implying that Cuba would remain socialist "*hasta la última gota de sangre*"—until the last drop of blood was spilled—as many revolutionary Cubans I spoke to asserted defiantly. But are socialism and capitalism necessarily diametrically opposed, or are there spaces of overlap? Must the choice be as stark as socialism or death?

When it is clarified that Marxist theory conceives of socialism as the evolutionary stage between capitalism and communism, one sees unequivocally that there are indeed spaces of overlap (Dirlik 1994; Gurley 1975). Communism is a utopian ideal in which "classes and social differences, as well as the state as an oppressive force, vanish" (Gurley 1975, 59). Because people exchange directly with one another so that material items lose their value-infused commodity status, there is no longer a need for money. (Of course, this ideal has never been achieved, even in the U.S.S.R.) Under socialism, in theory, money functions primarily as an incentive for workers to participate in production, rather than as a means of wealth accumulation (Verdery 1996, 182). Individuals with expendable money are perceived as "a challenge to governments that seek to maintain power by controlling the distribution of money" (Humphrey 1999, 45; see also Woodruff 1999).

To transform former capitalists into communists, the socialist phase requires a new value system that replaces self-interest with collective interests. Ernesto "Ché" Guevara, the primary architect of Cuba's new moral authority, contrasted capitalist motivations to the evolving socialist mode of thinking:

> It is not a matter of how many kilograms of meat one has to eat, or of how many times a year someone can go to the beach, or how many pretty things from abroad you might be able to buy with present-day wages. It is a matter of making the individual feel more complete, with much more inner wealth and much more responsibility.
>
> *(Guevara 1965)*

Most of the official organs of the Cuban government—including the Cuban Women's Federation (FMC), the Union of Communist Youth (UJC), and the Workers' Union (CTC)—served to develop their members' socialist consciousness. But also, the vanguard class stood apart from the general populace in their ready grasp of the new communist ideals mentioned above, and the state encouraged "socialist emulation" of this ideological elite. One revolutionary leader described the social differences that remain under socialism using the metaphor of the role of the fingers on the hand:

> No, señor, the doctor can never be the same and never get the same as, for example, a cowhand.... The doctor has another nivel, another status, recognized in society....No one is the same, not even in nature. Look, I have five fingers on my hand, and none of those five fingers are the same, but all are fingers.... There will always be something in the system that is not equal....
>
> *(Rosendahl 1997, 100–101)*

In the socialist stage, then, it is understood that some vestiges of inequality and material motivations required under capitalism remain because communism has not yet been accomplished.

This pragmatic capitalist loophole that socialism offers to communist doctrine is what has allowed the Cuban government to make such unorthodox moves as the wide-scale dollarization of the economy, acceptance of foreign investment, and opening to mass international tourism. The Cuban government believes the current "backwards" step on the path toward communism to be temporary—a Special Period of the Revolution. The government hopes it has finally found a way to guarantee a basic standard of living for its whole populace without excessive dependence on any one country, as it had depended on the Soviet Union before perestroika, and the United States and Spain in prior epochs (Jatar-Hausmann 1999).

After a thirty-year hiatus, Cuba has once again become a major tourist destination in the Caribbean. Despite the continuing four-decade U.S. blockade, through tourism Cuba has found its way into the post-Soviet global economy. In 2008, among Caribbean destinations (including Cancun, Mexico) only the Dominican Republic (2.15 million) received more foreign tourists than Cuba (1.21 million; Caribbean Tourism Organization 2009).

Post-socialist Globalization

> I used to sit out on the Malecón with my friends and we'd look up at the nightclub in the Habana Libre [hotel] and watch the lights flash. We'd just imagine what a good time people must be having....
> —*Yeshua, age 24*

If Cubans "race" tourists as *yumas* for whom the nation's scarce material resources are reserved, where does that leave everyday Cubans? The Cuban population has been promised the fruits of tourism's economic earnings in the form of continued socialist benefits; in the meantime, Cubans must—literally—sit outside while tourists enjoy those fruits (plentiful food and drink, immaculate spaces, rare medicines). Cuba's reentry into the global capitalist sphere has been problematic at both the individual and the national level.

Longtime Cuban president Fidel Castro once said, "We didn't like tourism very much...however, one of our tasks was to promote the development of tourism and prepare ourselves to withstand the inconveniences of tourism, since we couldn't live in a glass case" (Whittle 1997; see also Castro 1990). After having its economy underwritten by the Soviet Union for nearly three decades, Cuba was crushed by the fall of the Soviet Union and was forced to do business on the free market once again. While it may seem that relations with the Soviet Union protected Cuba from global relations, Cuba had many global links as a Soviet satellite, even if they were not capitalist in nature. Indeed, Cuba has been globalizing since the period when Arawakan Indian groups settled on the island from the South American mainland. Globalization involves increasing the flow of trade, finance, culture, ideas, and people brought about by technologies of communication and transportation (Appadurai 1996; Lewellen 2002). At the same time, globalization also involves local and regional adaptations to and resistances against these flows. What distinguishes today's post-Soviet globalization from the processes that have been ongoing for thousands of years in the form of transregional trade, pilgrimage, exploration, conquest, and colonialism is the focus on **neoliberal capitalism**.

Over time—especially from the period of European expansion in the sixteenth century—the economic role of the state has changed from the mercantilist one of controlling the national economy by protecting domestic industry from international competition to the more liberal one of maintaining a free or relatively free competitive market in which supply and demand (are supposed to) determine price. In practice, liberal states have protected private property, encouraged business, opened territory to corporate exploitation, and exerted military influence to protect overseas interests.

Liberalization implies the smooth and open movement of business around the world. When developing countries became dependent on international funding sources after the 1970s oil crisis,[4] international lending organizations like the IMF and the World Bank compelled them to use mechanisms that allowed for open (that is, without government regulation) capitalist trade with the broader capitalist West, especially so in the post-Soviet era. Before the neoliberal moment, developing nations had the objective of protecting themselves from international competition. Neoliberalism shifts the strategy for development from inward-oriented policies directed toward national self-sufficiency to outward-oriented policies designed for maximum integration into the global market; this implies the reduction and removal of tariffs and quotas and the elimination of barriers to foreign investment. Critics of neoliberalism argue that it has little sympathy for culturally specific contexts; it offers a single prescription regardless of the people or the place. Also, whereas the developed countries of the West liberalized incrementally over centuries, developing countries are experiencing (neo)liberalization rapidly and without much choice in the matter. While Cuba has reentered the global capitalist marketplace, a most notable reason to consider the Cuban case in the context of today's globalization is that, to date, it has survived the crisis of the post-Soviet Special Period without support from international lending organizations—even in face of the continuing U.S. blockade.

Methodology

The fieldwork that grounds this research was conducted in multiple sites of international tourism in Cuba, the bulk of it over an 18-month period between July 2000 and August 2003. I lived with a family in the Playa embassy district of Havana from July 2000 to June 2001, then made two- to four-week visits roughly every three months from October 2001 until August 2003, generally renting private rooms in the beach zone of Havana del Este. Additional weeklong visits were made in January and July 2004, July 2006, July 2007, and July 2008. The latter two fieldtrips to Central Havana are the sources of the updated data described in the epilogue.

More than half of my time was spent in the capital city of Havana, where the primary tourist attractions are architecture, beaches, and nightlife. I also studied in the niche tourism sites of Varadero (noted for its tourist-only beaches), Matanzas (where African-based religions are showcased for religious pilgrims), Santiago-de-Cuba (the birthplace of the revolution), Pinar del Rio (renowned for cigar-making), and Trinidad de Cuba (named a UNESCO World Heritage site for its colonial-era preservation). In each city, though I stayed in a hotel briefly each month to gain a firsthand perspective on the tourist experience (18 hotel stays in nine different hotels), I lived primarily in a *casa particular* (private home) with a family, participating in and observing day-to-day activities like grocery shopping, taking meals, traversing the city, watching television, and socializing. In this way, I was able to constantly analyze what it was like to live *a lo Cubano* (the Cuban way) in these regionally varied sites. In order to contrast home life with street life, I also spent a good part of each week participating in and observing Cuban–tourist interactions in places such as open-air souvenir markets, nightclubs, and Havana's Malecón seaside boardwalk. This kind of ethnographic research illuminated the ways Cubans perceived and treated foreigners—called *yumas*—as racially distinct, non-Cuban "Others." Because the research was concentrated in areas of high tourist volume, it does not focus significantly on Cuba's more rural regions; it does, however, capture the broad scope of tourism interactions in Cuba beyond the urban center of Havana.

In addition to **participant-observation**, my research methods included structured and unstructured interviews with both Cubans and tourists, and critical analyses of Cuban popular culture and practices. I conducted some one hundred unstructured interviews (fifteen recorded hours) with a racially and regionally diverse sampling of working-aged Cuban men and women. These informal interviews were designed to capture people's perceptions of tourists, of tourism as an industry, and of its relation to Cuba's revolutionary project. Further, I conducted in-depth life history interviews with ten individuals detailing changes in Cuban culture and society in relation to their lives (ten recorded hours). The interviews allowed Cubans to speak for themselves, without government-approved filtering. I also conducted semistructured interviews with fifty-six tourists (five recorded hours), addressing their reasons for travel to Cuba, their expectations beforehand, their experiences, and their revised impressions during their stay.

Finally, I analyzed Cuban popular culture and practice in such areas as music, dance, and bodily communication within sites of Cuban–tourist interaction (Byerly 1996; Reed 1998; Thomas 2002). While this book does not draw significantly from my textual analysis of popular music styles and lyrics (see Roland 2004), my translations of Cuban body language are interspersed throughout the ethnography. Also, in a few places, I reproduce colloquial Cuban expressions without providing an immediate or direct translation, leaving the reader to interpret the Cubanism in question from the broader discussion much in the way tourists must do (Thomas 2004).

All names used in this book are pseudonyms except for public officials speaking in public capacities. Except for the names of cities and key landmarks, place names (for example, hotels and nightclubs) are also pseudonyms.

In order to give readers a sense of the Cuban context, I use Spanish terms throughout the book; they are italicized in the text, and key terms are defined in the glossary. I have also italicized racial terms used in Cuba, like *negro* and *mulato*, in order to clarify that they refer to the Cuban context and not that of the United States. It will become clear that Cuba has a very complicated system of racial labels; I concentrate my explanation of Cuban race/color in the "Raciality in Cuba" section of chapter 2. While I use these terms throughout the book, I do not intend to reify them or imply that I, as an anthropologist, endorse the division of human beings by arbitrary physical features. In fact, because these labels are culturally constructed, I have tried to use, in describing individuals, (1) the terms they use for themselves, (2) the terms that I heard Cubans use for them, or (3) the terms I think Cubans would have used.

The Anthropological Eye/I

Cuban Color contains what some might consider an inordinate amount of **reflexivity**. I do not engage in the practice purely as self-indulgence, nor to diminish the role of my Cuban and other collaborators, but rather because as a foreigner studying foreignness and Cubanness I was often one of my own key informants. That is, my own experiences as a foreign person—though not quite a tourist—whose black and female body was often read to be Cuban—though I am not that either—provided me with data that I had to interpret just as I interpreted my interviews and observations. I do not write as the invisible observer, for I very seldom played that part during my fieldwork (Dubisch 1995; Galani-Moutafi 2000; Johnston 2001). My presence—black, female, and foreign—will likely be evident in my translations, as well as my interpretations of day-to-day observations—but so is that of any other anthropologist, whether they invoke the ethnographic "I" or not.

I should also note the unusual circumstance of having been married to one of my key interlocutors (see Pertierra 2007); he and his family—to whom I regularly refer as "my family"—also are highly visible in my readings of Cuba. "Yeshua" and I met during my first month of solo research in the summer of 2000, when he worked at the hotel where I lived. While I wrote up my notes poolside in the mornings, he regularly helped me make sense of the Cuban slang I was learning in "the streets" and also helped clarify many of the observations I had been making in Havana at large. The relationship took on romantic tones only at the very end of the month, after a long night of salsa dancing at a popular nightclub. We remained in regular contact until I returned to Cuba for my year of research in the summer of 2001. Yeshua was my boyfriend over the course of that year, during which his mother (Mami Teresa), aunt (Tía Caridad), and cousin (Hermina) became my surrogate family. Yeshua and I married one month after I completed my field research in 2002; we divorced one month after I had completed my doctorate in 2004.

During my research year, I frequently recorded our conversations—though I resisted my then fiancé's suggestion that I just keep the tape recorder rolling at all times; rather, I always kept it within arm's length (and always showed it to those present before visibly pressing the record button, with my eyebrow lifted in the *permiso*—may I?—question mark). As a (foreign) member of a Cuban household, I entered a space rarely visited by tourists. Sitting around the house, watching television with the family in one's underclothes to beat the insufferable heat is surely not the usual foreign—or anthropological—position. Still, though the family members were a key portal to my understanding of life in Cuba, they were not the focus of my research. Rather, because I spent so much time with them, they would often repeat things that had been stated (perhaps less cogently) in other interviews. Having heard the observation before, I could readily ask as many follow-up questions as I needed because the family speakers were so accessible to me. In other cases, a family member echoed an individual who, if quoted directly, would require an introduction that could lead readers astray from the point. Since the reader is already familiar with the family members, I occasionally use them to gloss other collaborators.

On the Ethics of Romantic Relationships in the Field

I was a happily single graduate student in my late twenties when I first traveled to Cuba for independent fieldwork in the summer of 2000. Though I had dated in the United States in the years before, only my intellectual interests could hold my attention for more than a few months at a time. I had no intention of developing any kind of romantic relationship while conducting my doctoral fieldwork.

But every fieldworker should know that relationships are required in order to conduct fieldwork. You can read beforehand, and you can observe until your wrists weary from taking notes, but in order to understand your research site, you have to talk to the people. And as master fieldworkers Bronislaw Malinowski (1922), Clifford Geertz (1973), and Paul Rabinow (1977) illustrate, "the people" will not tell you anything worth hearing unless your relationship is grounded in trust: that is, can they trust you, and can you trust them?

Female fieldworkers are trained to go into the field with backstories (true or fictional) of boyfriends or husbands back home, so that the men with whom they interact know they are "attached" to a male. Depending on my mood or my sense of the male with whom I was interacting, I sometimes engaged in this fiction. In Cuba, I was told on more than one occasion that "*no importa*"—my (imaginary) boyfriend didn't matter because "everyone needs more than one lover!" Truth be told, I felt as if I was on the reality television show *The Bachelorette* that summer, under constant romantic pursuit by security guards, hustlers, and foreign tourists too. Yeshua was the least likely of "winners," since we talked only at the hotel, especially in the mornings.

But Yeshua was different. The son of a die-hard revolutionary (and grandson of a man who was killed while working for a U.S. cattle rancher without compensation for his survivors), he bore strong animosity toward the United States and everything it represented; indeed, he called me the name "United States" for the first two weeks of my month at his hotel. I never felt pursued by him, so an easy friendship developed between us as he helped me with my fieldnotes. The music and heat of a night of dancing changed the nature of the relationship. In my last week in town, we began to "date" by going to fancy, high-priced places I couldn't afford. I felt that I was being hustled and told him so. We then shifted gears and began to schedule nightly meetings for conversation while we watched the sunset.

In the aftermath of our failed marriage, I have often wondered whether Yeshua was primarily interested in "hitting the jackpot" (as many Cubans described marrying a U.S. citizen and the prospect of legal emigration). Perhaps; but I am certain, too, that there was also love. I have also wondered whether Yeshua was the only one in our relationship who might have had ulterior motives: Soon after I returned to Cuba for long-term fieldwork in July 2001, he and I had a relationship-threatening disagreement that ended with his giving me an ultimatum. If we had been in the United States, I have no doubt that I would have allowed the relationship to end at that moment—but I can actually recall thinking, for one flashing instant, of what it would mean to conduct a year of fieldwork without his help (I am, by nature, a rather shy person, so speaking to strangers involves a high level of performance on my part). Our relationship continued through a myriad of ups and downs before our marriage and subsequent divorce. We now have a cordial and respect-filled friendship. But the question remains, did I parlay our relationship into a career? Perhaps, but—I repeat—I am certain there was also love.

Notes

1. I later learned that my (comparatively) expensive clothes and shoes were part of why I was identified as a prostitute, since sex work was presumed to be the only way a dark-complexioned woman could afford such obviously foreign goods. Also, my dreadlocks were read as braided extensions, a popular hairstyle among black sex workers.

2. Whereas in many Latin American contexts, *mestizo* means having mixed white and indigenous ancestry, in Cuba, where the native peoples were exterminated relatively early in the colonial period, the term usually denotes an indeterminate racial mixture.

3. As I clarify later, blackness is a negative identity in the Cuban context, so many individuals of known African ancestry choose "softer" terms on the black–white racial continuum. While the national symbol is *La Mulata* (a female of African and European ancestry), Cuban national identity—as exemplified in politics, the media, and my own interview responses—is largely *mestizo* (whitened racially indeterminate male).

4. From October 1973 to March 1974, OPEC refused to sell oil to the United States and other countries that supported Israel in the Yom Kippur war. Oil and gas prices remained inflated through the 1980s.

CHAPTER 2

"Blackness" and Race Matters in Cuba

I don't know how I look to you, through your eyes....You've seen how we live....But *you don't really know me unless you know my past*. There were what, six of us? My two aunts, my mother, us twins, then Angela....There wasn't always enough food, and sometimes we'd eat only one meal a day....And there used to be such racism here....There were the clubs (*lycees*) that we couldn't go to—there were clubs for whites and clubs for blacks. For every group....The police used to stop us and say we couldn't walk on the white walkways, so I asked where should I [a *mulata*] walk? Oh, how I dreamed I'd be a lawyer one day....But those were just dreams, because back in those days, there was no way....

And then came the revolution and everything changed. I told you before that we didn't even have electricity in Jiguaní until our revolution, right? Then I went and lived up in the mountains with the Literacy Campaign. I felt I had finally served my time in service to the revolution after seven years as chief of the Literacy Brigade. Then one day, a few years ago, two men approached me out here on Reina [Avenue].[1] One was big and black and the other was *mulato*. They almost backed me against the wall and I was scared. But they greeted me as *Maestra* and said they remembered me from the mountains. They told me they had just come back from the Soviet Union, where they had completed a course in electrical engineering. I was overcome with emotion and I started to cry right there! I knew I had made a difference in their lives. So that's what our revolution's about. I may not have much, but inside I'm content. I'm satisfied. When I look back on my life, I've come such a long way and it is much better. The revolution has brought both quantitative and qualitative change. Now we have free education for everyone, so [my daughter] Hermina and [nephew] Yeshua had the opportunities that they've had. Without that, they'd be nothing.

—*Maria Caridad, age 62 [emphasis added]*

In this passage from an interview, Tía Caridad reflects on her life before the revolution in order to explain why she, like so many others, continues to celebrate and support the Cuban revolution. Though there was a tendency among my interviewees not to talk much about the revolution prior to the Special Period beyond saying things were "*normal*" back then, there is sufficient literature on the era to sketch some aspects of that normative revolutionary life (Pérez 1988; Pérez-Stable 1993; Rosendahl 1997).

The 1960s were heady times in socialist Cuba, as the society was restructured in ways that removed the key economic, cultural, and military roles the United States had played since the turn of the twentieth century. In quick succession, the United States enforced an embargo on Cuba for nationalizing American properties, while the revolutionaries sought the military backing of the Soviet Union and declared their movement socialist. With the subsequent departure of Cuba's elite classes into exile, a primary objective of the revolution was to raise the standard of living for the poor, largely uneducated masses. The vast majority of the population enthusiastically participated in building the socialist society of *Hombres Nuevos* (New Men and Women) through a variety of social movements, including the aforementioned literacy campaigns. The nationwide effort to harvest 10 million tons of sugar late in the decade is a notable failure that—while resulting in a record 8.5 million tons—also left the economy overly focused on that target (see Pérez 1988). Revolutionary aspirations for greater political and economic independence ended with increased reliance on the USSR.

For the next two decades, Cuba was dependent on its membership with the Soviet Union's Council for Mutual Economic Assistance (CMEA, also called COMECON), in which underdeveloped member states (Cuba, Mongolia, and Vietnam) traded their available resources (like Cuba's sugar) for products provided by more industrially developed member states (like Russian oil) at rates far below their market value. Until the late 1980s, this CMEA subsidy allowed Cubans an artificially high standard of living based on imported Soviet goods that were disseminated through the centralized state system. Given this supply-driven economic system—as well as the extent of rationing—households occasionally had more money than available items to spend it on (Rosendahl 1997). In contrast to the post-Soviet Special Period during which I conducted my research, these were the revolution's "good old days."

While I analyze the generational implications of the revolution in chapter five, here I extend Tía Caridad's opening words—"you don't really know me unless you know my past"—to Cuba more broadly. This chapter briefly outlines Cuban history (see the "Timeline" at the end of the book) in order to deconstruct Cuban understandings of race that form the foundations of today's racialized tourist interactions.

Raciality in Cuba

The Cuban construction of race is defined by three closely related features. The first involves the origins of race mixture and the role of *mulato*-ness in a white-aspiring society. The second involves the political significance of Cuba's racial democracy myth. And the third involves how race is understood to extend beyond skin color. Though these cultural features endure, a close examination reveals that they have also evolved and changed over time.

From the early days of slavery—which began in Cuba upon conquest in 1512 and ended at the late date of 1886—throughout Latin America, race was never understood in purely black-vs.-white terms. Because there were very few women from Europe in the early colony, many European men engaged in sexual relations with their black slaves and indentured native women servants, creating the intermediate categories of *mulatos* and *mestizos*, respectively. From the beginning, then, Latin American ideas about race implied the sexuality of women of color and white male empowerment. By the time family settlement to the Americas was encouraged by the Spanish colonial government in the late eighteenth century, white men had already established a practice of relative acceptance toward their racially mixed offspring, who, at least statistically, swelled their ranks, thereby bolstering their power. Many of these individuals became Cuba's free people of color; depending on their complexion or social class, some could legally enter the ranks of whites in a practice called *blanqueamiento* or "whitening" (see Martinez-Alier 1974). These exceptional cases gave hope to their darker, lower class countrymen and women that race mixture could lead to social advancement.

The problem with the whitening ideal is that it was contingent upon the simultaneous darkening of lighter groups. Between the seventeenth and nineteenth centuries, the Spanish court issued numerous royal decrees that sought to protect whiteness by inscribing interracial marriage rules. White Cuban families frequently protested the intermarriage of their children with darker persons in an effort to protect their "purity of blood" (a legal argument supported early in the colonial period that sought to protect the lineage of nobles). In one nineteenth-century court case, an official denied an interracial marriage petition on the grounds that "...their offspring would pertain to one of those undefined and so common and awkward castes, who neither want to mix with the *pardos* whom they scorn nor are accepted by the white, by whom they themselves are disdained in turn" (Martinez-Alier 1974, 18).

In the past, scholars of race in the Latin American and Caribbean context often observed the social distinctions between blacks and browns/*mulatos* and concluded that brownness formed a separate entity between blackness and whiteness (Degler 1971; Heuman 1981; Wright 1990). In contrast, Aline Helg (1995) argues that Cuba's racial history is different from other Latin American contexts in that the free blacks and *mulatos* joined forces very early in the struggle for emancipation, recognizing their common outsider status vis-à-vis the whites:

> Cuba's social construct of race is remarkable in Latin America and the Caribbean in that for almost one hundred years Cubans have perpetuated the mid-nineteenth century notion of a *raza de color* (race of color) or *clase de color* (class of color) without differentiating mulattoes from blacks and have often referred to both *pardos* (mulattoes) and **morenos** (blacks) as *negros* (black).
>
> *(Helg 1995, 3)*

Helg argues that *pardos* (browns) were understood to be nonwhites and associatively *negros* at least in the eyes of whites in power. In this way, race described not only phenotypical differentiation, but also a commonality of position. Central, then, to conceptions of race in Cuba is that the sites of privilege—the upper classes, the politically and socially empowered, the culturally refined—are all associated with whiteness or whitening, while blackness is associated with absence of privilege—the lower classes, the politically and positionally disempowered, those with a "low cultural level." I draw from Helg's explanation in my use of racial terminology throughout the book. In accordance with Cuban usage—and for ease of understanding by students in the United States—I frequently use the English term "black" to describe Cubans of African descent who would be classified as *negro* in Cuba, though in specific instances the term may also be used for those considered *mulatos*. Likewise, I use "white" to describe the broad category that incorporates those Cubans identified as *blanco* or *mestizo*.

As was the case elsewhere in the Americas, in Cuba blackness became equated with lowliness from the inception of mass enslavement in the sixteenth century. Along with members of Cuba's indigenous

Ciboney-Arawak, Taino-Arawak, and Carib populations who survived military conquest and exposure to European diseases, the slaves worked in the early sugar mills located primarily in eastern Cuba—the center of economic and political life at the time.

However, from the late sixteenth century, when Spain's attention turned to gold prospects on the American mainlands, the fledgling plantation economies in the Spanish Caribbean were essentially neglected until the late 1700s. As a result, the remaining Spanish, indigenous, and African residents lived for nearly a century largely outside the crown's structures of control. These early residents became Cuba's earliest **creole** population of *guajiros*—land-based peasants who had intermixed to such an extent that they did not readily fit into the *negro*, *blanco*, or *mulato* categories. Still, because skin color was believed to signify one's nearness to slavery, social hierarchy within the group was based on a light-to-dark color continuum (Hoetink 1985). Colonial-era marriage norms reiterate this point: "'All men should endeavour to advance instead of regress,' advance both in relation to one's colour by 'whitening' oneself and in terms of one's distance from slavery. The lighter the skin and the further removed from slavery, the greater the chances of ascending the social ladder" (Martinez-Alier 1974, 93). The whitening ideal, then, is believed to result in the material and social benefits of whiteness.

Cuban Meanings of Marriage

Like race and gender, marriage is a cultural construct. In Spain, for example, marriage sought to specify a child's maternal and paternal lineage for the purposes of inheritance. In colonial Cuba, the lower classes (regardless of race) may have aspired toward the stable and secure future offered by this Western marriage model, but Spanish cultural influence was not all-encompassing. When the Spanish neglected the Caribbean from the early 1500s through late 1700s, what has been called a "Caribbean" family structure arose in Cuba (Rosendahl 1997). The dearth of priests in residence led to common-law marriages, which could dissolve with relative ease. Later, the mass importation of African slaves also brought West African cultural practices in which a man could take multiple wives, even if he was not legally married to any of them. Among the elite classes, white men formed unofficial unions and had children with concubines of lower social class and darker skin. These marriage models predominated in Cuba from the colonial period through the Republican era of the 1950s (Hoetink 1985; Martinez-Alier 1974; Rosendahl 1997; Stoner 1991). The general result was both considerable racial mixing and a cultural imperative to marry someone whiter than oneself in order to "whiten" one's children. Even after several centuries, the whitening ideal remains. Narrating her life-history entitled *Reyita* to her daughter, María de los Reyes Castillo Bueno reflects back to 1923:

> One day I knelt down clutching her image [the Virgin of Charity of El Cobre] and asked her for a good, hard-working, white husband, without a family that would be ashamed of me for being black. I know you understand why I wanted to marry a white man...in those days, marrying white was vital.... [When I introduced my mother to my new husband] Isabel was very pleased, in the first place because he was white and her grandchildren weren't going to be dark black; she congratulated me for having understood the importance of improving the race, and secondly, because my life would become stable.
>
> *(Castillo Bueno 2000, 59, 62)*

With the revolution's significant reforms in racial, gender, and class ideologies, one irony of today's post-Soviet era is a return to these colonial-era patterns of gender relations. The economic hardships of the Special Period have again led women to seek a more secure future through exogenous (outgroup) associations with high-status men—now, with foreign tourists.

Cuban Independence?

By the middle of the nineteenth century, having secured their new wealth largely through trade with their neighbor to the north—the new nation of the United States—many among the white creole elite began to rally for Cuba's independence from Spain. A key question for those who pressed for autonomy was the rights of Cuba's significant black population.

> Planters reacted with horror to the circumstances attending the abolition of slavery in the United States. The enormously destructive conflict...persuaded them that emancipation should be undertaken from above, peacefully, gradually, and with indemnification to owners—not from below, through war, suddenly, and without compensation. After the mid-1860s, one other consideration influenced creole thinking: any hope of future annexation with the United States was now contingent on the abolition of slavery.
>
> *(Pérez 1988, 114)*

With the experience of both the Haitian revolution and the U.S. Civil War within living memory for some, many planters had to be convinced that independence from Spain would not unleash undesirable social forces: Might the white elite lose control of the (former) slaves, as occurred in Haiti? Might they lose everything, as occurred for many U.S. plantation holders?

FIGURE **2.1**   Antonio Maceo (courtesy of HistoryofCuba.com)

When the Ten Years' War—the first Cuban war for independence—began in 1868, slaveholder Carlos Manuel de Céspedes addressed the question of slave emancipation by freeing all of his slaves. As a leader of the separatists, Céspedes declared that all slave owners who joined the revolution could be compensated for their slaves by the new government upon the defeat of the Spanish. The slaves would be drafted into military service as *mambises* (revolutionary fighters); indeed, by the end of the war, many former slaves would prove themselves to be valiant soldiers and be recognized as national heroes—among them, the *mulato* General Antonio Maceo (Helg 1995; de la Fuente 2001; see Figure 2.1). Throughout the Ten Years' War, both Cuba and Spain promised the eventual abolition of slavery, but the war ended in February 1878 with a small group negotiating the Treaty of Zanjón that freed only those slaves who had fought in the war. Maceo and many other *mambises* remained dissatisfied. With the question of full emancipation still outstanding, Spain eventually sought to gain favor with the blacks by freeing all the remaining slaves through a royal decree in 1886. Nonetheless, many revolutionaries continued to agitate for full independence until the outbreak of the second war for independence in 1895.

José Martí is perhaps the most famous Cuban patriot (see Figure 2.2). An activist born in Cuba in 1853 of a Spanish father and a Cuban mother, Martí spent over half his life in exile because of his anticolonial writings.

FIGURE 2.2   José Martí (courtesy of HistoryofCuba.com)

From New York, Martí founded the Cuban Revolutionary Party (PRC) in 1892 with the objective of toppling Spanish colonialism. Pointing to the multiracial deaths in service to the aspiring nation, the PRC promoted a platform of antiracism and raceless Cuban nationality (Ferrer 1999). Martí also warned that Spain was not the only colonial entity of which Cuba should beware. In his famous "Our America" essay written during the first independence war (1868–1878), he suggested that the United States also posed a threat to Cuban political and economic sovereignty (Martí 1977):

> But our America may also face another danger. . . . The hour is near when she will be approached by an enterprising and forceful nation that will demand intimate relations with her, though it does not know her and disdains her. And virile nations self-made by the rifle and the law love other virile nations, and love only them.
>
> *(Martí 1977, 93)*

Martí's forewarnings about the imperialist intentions of the United States were only too accurate. Despite hesitations about incorporating Cuba's large black population into the U.S. state structure, the United States had long expressed interest in purchasing Cuba from Spain (Ferrer 1999; Helg 1995; Pérez 1988). As the war waned and Cuba was on the brink of defeating Spain, in February 1898 the U.S.S. Maine—a warship sent by

President William McKinley to protect U.S. properties in Cuba during the war—exploded in the Havana harbor. Accusing the Spaniards,[2] the U.S. entered the war, and what had been a three-decade war for Cuban independence became known in U.S. history books as the five-month "Spanish-American War."

Cubans won little with the American victory. Though the 1898 Teller Amendment recognized Cuban sovereignty, the Platt Amendment of 1901, which was forcibly incorporated into the new Cuban constitution, effectively made Cuba a U.S. protectorate: "the United States may exercise the right to intervene for the preservation of Cuban independence, [and] the maintenance of a government adequate for the protection of life, property, and individual liberty" (Ruíz 1968, 24). Having occupied much of the land ravaged in the decades of war, by 1906, U.S. interests owned many of Cuba's resources—from sugar mills to the electric companies—with the result that the U.S. military and political apparatus intervened in Cuban affairs several times before the abrogation of the Platt Amendment in 1934.

While many who had fought in the Cuban independence movement had believed they were fighting for a Cuba that had no need for racial classifications, the new nation's political and economic intermarriage with the United States during the height of Jim Crowism reinforced many white Cubans' longstanding resistance to antiracism. Faced with constant scrutiny by U.S. officials concerning their ability to govern themselves, the Cuban ruling class sought to demonstrate that they, too, possessed such marks of civilization as "refinement, civility, and whiteness" (Ferrer 1999, 191). As one Cuban politician stated in 1916: "Coming out of slavery a few short years ago ... [the colored race] has not been able to give to civilization more than a handful of talents ... Slavery ... [and] the colonial system left in the agitated soul of the man of color, the pernicious trace of all ills" (de la Fuente 2001, 30). With deficiencies that included a "lack of education and work habits, and a 'bad moral status,'" white Cubans blamed blacks—and their inability to rid themselves of the effects of slavery—for their own societal exclusion (de la Fuente 2001, 30). In the early twentieth century, whites—even the Spanish former enemies—were promoted to high-level posts, while many of the blacks who had previously held high military rank in the service of Cuban nationhood were demoted to positions deemed appropriate for their race in police stations or post offices (Helg 1995).

A number of black and *mulato* veterans were dissatisfied with the new nation's shortcomings. In 1910, one hundred of these men—claiming a following of some two thousand others—decided to form a political party with the hope of achieving a modicum of political and economic power through the democratic process. The most prominent opposition to the *Partido Independiente de Color* (Independent Colored Party/PIC) was led by Senator Martín Morua—himself a man of color—who in 1912 proposed a law, based on Martí's myth of racial equality, that forbade political parties to form along racial lines. When the PIC refused to disband and, in 1912, opted to follow a white veteran group's earlier model of armed protest, a white militia randomly massacred thousands of black men, regardless of their political affiliations (Helg 1995; Rolando 2001). With that crushing blow, "blacks were forced to silently accept their lot or immediately [be] labeled as racist and antipatriotic" (Helg 1995, 245).

Mainstreaming Black Culture

Though Cubans of color found the political avenue to full participation in the national project closed to them, they nonetheless had a significant impact at the level of national culture. Much to their chagrin, however, it was not the white-aspiring culture of the black middle class, but rather the African-inspired music, dance, and religions of Cuba's most marginalized blacks and *mulatos* that would come to signify Cubanness. Despite protests and hesitations by Cuba's elite—white and nonwhite—as more U.S. Americans vacationed in their Cuban playground during Prohibition (1920s) and, after the Great Depression, in the 1940s and 1950s, black Cuban culture increasingly became equated with mainstream Cuban culture in the eyes of foreign tourists, and eventually by Cubans themselves (R. Moore 1997; Pérez 1999; Schwartz 1997).

In the aftermath of the wars for independence and emancipation, few professions were open to blacks and *mulatos* in the early Republic. Because whites looked down upon the arts as a profession, entertainment became one means for *negros* and *mulatos* to earn a living legitimately. Many became conservatory-trained musicians, skilled in European musical styles like *danzón* or *trova*. This did not mean they may not also have a background in African-derived musical genres from their home environments. While bands could experiment with African rhythms and percussion instruments for audiences in their own neighborhoods, drums were explicitly disallowed in many elite and middle-class establishments through the 1930s (R. Moore 1997). Ironically, American tourists who wandered off the beaten tourist path in search of "authentic" Cuban culture and heard these kinds of performances are largely responsible for bringing Afro-Cuban culture out of the shadows and into the mainstream (see Figure 2.3). In an effort to recapture the authenticity-seeking segment of their audience, taverns and cabarets began to promote black music

FIGURE 2.3   Rumba performers (author's postcard collection)

forms. As the black cultural heritage was validated by its own 1930s black arts movement that paralleled the Negritude movements occurring world-wide during that period (including the Harlem Renaissance in the United States), Cubans eventually came to embrace aspects of it like *rumba* and *Santería* as a significant part of their national heritage.

The historical processes outlined to this point—African enslavement in sustenance of a sugar-based economy, an independence movement that promised national autonomy and racial equality, the subsequent failure of both of those promises in the shadows of U.S. imperial occu-pation, and the emergence of black cultural forms as Cuban national culture—form part of the background to understanding the construct of race in the context of today's post-Soviet revolutionary project in Cuba. The constant refrain that *el color no importa* (color doesn't matter) in Cuba has its roots in Morua's Law, which presupposed a factual basis for José Martí's hypothetical Cuban racial democracy. The 1912 mas-sacre of thousands of men of color forced future generations of blacks and *mulatos* to silently accept this mythology as national doctrine or risk making themselves targets again. While Cuba's socialist revolution has gone a long way toward rectifying several sources of past inequities, many underlying racial beliefs remain intact. Those racial stereotypes and prejudices are being magnified in today's era of revived international tourism.

Race and the Revolution

Historians widely agree that the seeds of the 1959 Cuban revolution were sown upon the conclusion of the nineteenth-century wars for independence (Pérez 1988; Pérez-Stable 1993; Ruíz 1968; R. Smith 1979), when aspirations toward autonomy were suddenly dashed by the U.S. intervention in the war effort and then by the Platt Amendment that established Cuba as politically and economically dependent on the United States. Cuba's Republican era (1902–1940) featured a series of puppet administrations that catered to U.S. interests more than to the needs of the poor, illiterate masses throughout the country. However, with the adoption of a new constitution in 1940—which excluded the widely resented Platt Amendment—a new wave of nationalist sentiment began to spread throughout the country. Fulgencio Batista, a *mulato adelantado* (whitened; see Figure 2.4, later) military officer who rose to power by securing the backing of U.S. presidents, was legally elected president from 1940 to 1944 in the first Constitutional administration.

Around this time many university students became interested in the writings of José Martí—previously unpopular because of their anti-U.S. sentiment. Indeed, two of the major political parties that would soon emerge were called the *Ortodoxos* and the *Auténticos*, signifying their respectively envisioned "orthodox" or "authentic" interpretations of Martí's teachings. As a member of the Orthodox party, the young Fidel Castro was attracted not only to the message of Cuba for the Cubans, but also to Martí's humanist plea for social justice. In 1952, when Batista angered much of the nation's proud citizenry by instituting a coup only months before national elections were to take place, Fidel Castro's name was on the ballot for a senatorial seat. In July 1953, Castro and a group of fellow intellectual rebels attempted to overthrow Batista by attacking a military installation—the Moncada barracks—in Santiago-de-Cuba. The rebels were caught and imprisoned. However, the speech Castro delivered in his trial defense—known as "History Will Absolve Me" (Castro 1975)—became the platform of the revolution once the rebels regrouped after being released from prison in a 1955 general amnesty. When Castro and his band of rebels eventually overthrew Batista, the revolution took on a social justice program that aimed to improve the conditions of the poorest and most marginalized citizens—and among this group were Cuba's *raza de color* (people of color).

As whites left the country by the planeload—especially after the revolution was pronounced socialist in character in 1961—the dearth of professionals at all levels drew attention to the need to restructure the educational system (see Pérez 1988). The Federation of Cuban Women (FMC) mobilized thousands of young women with at least a secondary education (like Tía Caridad) to help their illiterate countrymen and women learn basic reading skills through a massive literacy campaign. By the end of the 1961 Year of Education, the adult literacy rate was reportedly 96 percent, "the highest in Latin America and one of the highest in the world" (Pérez 1988, 359). The army of prostitutes who had served tourists from the U.S. were reeducated and given more socially acceptable service sector jobs as clerks, bus drivers, and waitresses (Fusco 1998).

The FMC was also central in the campaign to revitalize the marital institution through a new Family Code. Mass wedding ceremonies were held to legalize longtime common-law unions. Divorce laws were liberalized, so that women were not confined to relationships that were abusive or otherwise undesirable. Women were free to make choices about their bodies and themselves independently of their husbands.

Most alarming to the white elite were the changes to secondary education: in order to promote the revolution's integrationist policies, older teenage students were sent to boarding schools in rural areas, away from the potentially racist influences of their parents and grandparents.[3] The revolution promised that any qualified student could receive higher education free of charge. Youths from the countryside flooded the University of Havana until regional universities were opened throughout the country. Since the 1970s, remarkable numbers of blacks, *mulatos*, and women have become professionals in such previously exclusive fields as medicine and engineering (Casal 1979; Pérez 1988). In order to minimize discriminatory hiring practices, jobs have been allocated by central agencies since 1960 (de la Fuente 2001).

The revolution has certainly made great strides in integrating recreational facilities and workplaces—the two areas Castro identified as the primary sites of racial discrimination. Critics argue, however, that this limited understanding of the manifestations of racism continues to gloss over black and *mulato* experiences. Because even after some 50 years of revolution blacks are not represented proportionately in politics at the national level, their interests continue to be defined by others (C. Moore 1988, 2008; Sawyer 2006). Moreover, as is the case throughout the Americas, unless blacks make their identities and behaviors conform to white norms, their exclusion from the political process can be attributed to their own cultural backwardness rather than to systemic racism (R. Moore 1997).

From Black(ness) to White(ned)

Aqui, no hay nada de raza. We're all the same. I've got a little bit of everything in me. *Llevo negro esclavo, español, indio—llevo todo!* Just like my grandchildren—you see these here, but I've also got a nephew who is **prieto**, prieto, prieto! But how adorable he is!

—Saida, age 80

For a people who claim not to assign import to skin color, Cubans invoke terms that refer to phenotypical distinctions with striking frequency in the course of ordinary conversation. In the preceding quote, my eighty-year-old neighbor explains that "race is a nonissue" in Cuba, citing her own racial composite of "black slave, Spanish, and Indian" as an example. Still, as she contrasts the *mestizo* offspring with whom she lived to her nephew who is "*very*, very dark!" one cannot help but notice the exceptionalism of his being both "dark" and "adorable." Both Cuban history and today's Cuban racial terminology show a pattern in which, in general, blackness and black identifying features are denigrated in comparison to whiteness or features identified as "whitened." Even in the narrative that opened this chapter, Tía Caridad's initial fear of her former students is clearly linked to their skin colors.

Figure 2.4 illustrates a sampling of the broad range of race and color terms used today in Cuba (and elsewhere in Latin America). The *blanco* or "white" category links race almost exclusively to hair color, with the significant exceptions of olive-skinned *trigueños*, who have straight black hair, and *lechosos*, who have a complexion described as "milky white." The different gradations of *negro* and *mulato*—featuring dark and light color variants and also considering hair texture and facial features—address the extent of discernible African ancestry. What may appear from behind to be a *trigueña* with straight black hair and naturally tanned arms may be revealed a *mulata clara* when her full lips or nose are visible. Significantly, members of what was explained to me as a "special category" of *mulato* called *jaba(d)o* may have any of the lighter complexions—including *lechoso*—often with hazel, blue, or green eyes, but are considered nonwhite because they have some prominent "black" feature, most notably *pasas* ("nappy" or what is called "bad" hair). (In the United States, many *jaba(d)os* would be described as "able to pass" for white.) There is also a "special category" of *negro* called *moro* that includes dark complexioned people with what is considered "good" hair texture—resembling North African Moors.

In addition to these terms that refer to phenotypical features, there are also relational uses of racial terms that imply familiarity. Within any Cuban household—black or white—the darkest member is often referred

> **BLANCO**
> *Rubio* = Blonde
> *Lechoso* = Milky white
> *Pelirojo* = Red head
> *Castaño (Claro→Oscuro)* = (Light→Dark) Brunette
> *Trigueño* = Olive complexion w/ straight black hair
> ↑
> **MULATO**
> *Adelantado/"De salir"* = Advancing (into whiteness)
> *Claro→Oscuro* = Light→Dark complexioned
> *Jaba(d)o* = Negroid and European features (esp. hair/eyes)
> ↑
> **NEGRO**
> *Adelantado/"De salir"* = Advancing (into *mulato*-ness)
> *Moro* = Dark complexion/straight hair
> *Claro→Oscuro* = Light→Dark complexioned
> *Azul* = "Blue" black

FIGURE 2.4   The race–color continuum

to affectionately as *"negro/a."* A white *castaño* Cuban-American high school student, who was born in Havana, fondly reminisced, "My grandmother used to hug me and call me *'mi negro.'* ..." Only after it was repeatedly explained to me within my Cuban family that the term was meant "lovingly" and not as a slur did I eventually cease months of protesting being called *"Negra"* or *"Negri"* (a shortened form of *Negrita*) as though it were my name. Still, I recognized the significance of status in such usages when María Teresa, a 62-year-old *jaba(d)a*, was relaying a story about her ex-husband, who is classified racially as *negro*. When telling a story in her husband's voice, she repeatedly referred to herself as "Negra," to which each time her niece quietly corrected "Mulata"—apparently concerned that I might not distinguish Mami's race and status from the color of her skin.

As Peter Wade (1993) explains the common Latin American phenomenon, my family nickname was Negra because it is "a friendly term of address to people easily classifiable as 'black'" and "intimacy is implied by the ability to use a potentially derogatory term without derogation" (260). When María Teresa—a blue-eyed *mulata*—was called "Negra" by her husband, the term of endearment also conveyed the power differential between men and women that parallels that between whites and blacks. In this case, "the connotations are of intimacy but also of paternalism, dependence, and service" (260). And the white *castaño* high school student was called *negro* by his grandmother because he was a junior family member—the implicit hierarchical difference was age. Wade summarizes, "Negro, then, may not convey disrespect, but its various meanings as a term of address are underlain by a central concept of lower position on a hierarchical scale" (Wade 1993, 260). These examples show how a biologically or ancestrally based "race" can be detached from black bodies and relationally applied to close friends, female lovers, and younger family members without undermining the fixed meanings about the lowly status of blackness in comparison to whiteness. Because such terms are so flexibly applied—and because of the racial democracy myth—Cubans generally do not recognize them as racial at all.

Perhaps more telling about the construction of race in Cuba than the broad range of terms are their progressive or "evolutionary" usages. Just as the arrows in Figure 2.4 that point upwards from blackness toward whiteness symbolize the perceived "advancement" of the Cuban people through historic policies of *blanqueamiento* (whitening), within each non-white category there is a "subrace" of "*adelantados*"—literally, advancers, that is, into the next category up—also called "*de salir.*" *De salir* translates as "leaving from," so the person described could be thought of as "leaving" blackness or *mulato*-ness. For example, Yeshua—the chestnut-brown complexioned son of a *jaba(d)a* and a *negro*—once explained to me that he considers himself *negro*, though owing to both his soft hair texture and his mild manners, people generally refer to him alternately as a *negro adelantado* or a *mulato oscuro*. But Nadine Fernández (1996) submits an alternate meaning of *de salir*—that the black or *mulato* is "good enough" to accompany in public despite his or her biological heritage. I, for instance, am a dark-complexioned *negra* who was accepted by my fair complexioned in-laws largely because they saw me as a *negra de salir* owing to my high level of education and "cultural refinement." This alternate meaning speaks to the possibility in Cuba, and elsewhere in Latin America, that one may be socially accepted as though one were white (or *mulato*) depending on one's position in society (Wade 1993). In other words, skin color and ancestry are not the only determinants of race; such class-based considerations as property ownership, occupation, and education also come into play, as elsewhere in the Caribbean and in North America. Javier once told me a popular story that illustrates this Cuban racial construction:

There was a dark-skinned doctor who had married a white woman. When the newlywed couple reached her parents' house in the countryside, she went in first. They asked her who the black man driving the car was, "the chauffeur?" She said, "No, he's my husband." The

parents cursed and raised a fuss until she told them "He's a doctor";
then they ran out and embraced him, saying, "Oh, our son!"

In *Nationalizing Blackness*, Robin Moore (1997) sheds light on not only
the policy of racial or physical whitening but also aspirations for cultural
whitening. He explains that, rather than strictly following the Darwinian
(or biological) evolutionary race model (see chapter 1), in the early decades
of the twentieth century the newly independent, racially mixed nations of
Latin America, including Cuba, came to prefer the cultural evolution school
of thought that conceived of blacks and whites as potential equals, though
blacks' "traditions and modes of behavior were [still thought to be] influenced
by earlier stages of cultural development" (R. Moore 1997, 32). From this perspective, blacks could be equal to whites if they would only Westernize. In
this way, the lower sectors of society were motivated to "improve" themselves
culturally. That is, they were encouraged to forsake norms and behaviors
associated with the African-descended blacks of the lower classes and instead
adopt the European standards and mores of the upper classes in such cultural areas as religion, speech, music, and dance. Both *blancos* and *negros*, at
least conceptually, could slide up and down this cultural scale.

Today, under a revolution that purports to have eliminated both racism and classism, those same Eurocentric premises that assume that "white
is right" nevertheless continue to define an individual's cultural designa-
tion. Nadine Fernández (1996) explains that "culture, in this sense, implies
a social hierarchy: one group with high culture (*más nivel, alta cultura*)
and the other group with low culture (*menos nivel, bajo* [sic] *cultura*)."
Specifically, **nivel de cultura** alludes to an individual's (or their family's
or community's) "level of formal education, public manners and etiquette,
and...degree of social refinement" (Fernández 1996, 147). Because "'high
culture' is associated most often with whites, while 'low culture' connotes
poverty and blackness," this socially relative understanding of culture is
also raced (Fernández 1996, 147).

While this link between *cultura* and race is historically based, I heard
similar articulations in my contemporary conversations: "I normally don't
speak to people of *baja cultura* [because] blacks are the ones who don't
want to work but who want everything....I'm not saying only blacks are
of *cultura baja*, but most of them are and most whites are of a higher cultural level." My sense that comments like this one by university-educated
Hermina, a *jaba(d)a*, had racist connotations was validated by Javier, also
jaba(d)o but Rastafarian: "Look, I know my fellow Cubans. And people
like them look at people like me as being of *baja cultura*. They think of me
as black, uneducated, and poor—like they're so much better than we are."

Despite the revolution's attempts to level the social playing field, revolutionary leaders admit that they have not been able to mandate away long-standing beliefs about race. In that regard, on one occasion, Yeshua—who self-identifies as *negro*—commented that he did not like to see groups of young black and *mulato* men hanging around in his neighborhood: "That's the reason there are so many black men in jail—no good can come of it." I countered that it was likely that kind of prejudice that leads to disproportionate black imprisonment in both Cuba and the United States. Skin color, social status, and cultural behaviors (that is, acting more or less "cultured") continue to influence the perception of an individual's race.

Gendered Race/Raced Gender

Much of Cuba's racially democratic discourse gains credence from founding father José Martí's assertion that Cuban nationalism transcended race because both black and white Cubans (men) fought and died for independence from Spain (Ferrer 1999). If the Cuban race was founded through the "fraternal embrace" across racial lines described by Martí, then black and *mulata* women's "(e)raced" bodies are the sites of the physical and social violations at the origins of Cuba's now celebrated racially mixed heritage (see Kutzinski 1993).

The Mulata has her origins as a Cuban national symbol in the urban centers of the late nineteenth century, as the nation was becoming independent and slavery was being abolished. She is a complex character who symbolizes the ideal of race mixture and whitening, female beauty and sexuality, but also women's innate Eve-like treachery and untrustworthiness. In fact, Cuba's patron saint, Nuestra Señora de la Caridad del Cobre (Our Lady of the Charity of the Copper Mine; see Figure 2.5), is generally represented as a *mulata* whose Yoruba incarnation in Santería, Oshún, is characterized in terms that parallel discourse on the Mulata symbol:

> Ochún in Cuba is most popularly imaged as a *mulata*, a woman of mixed race who lives between the world of black and white, at once both and neither....Perhaps it is in reference to her image as a *mulata* that Ochún is conceived as a flirt, courtesan or prostitute. Mixed-race women occupied a peculiar niche in colonial Cuban society where they might achieve a level of social prominence, financial independence, and upward mobility for their children if they became official mistresses of wealthy Cuban white men....The love of such women could never be self-determining and so their gracious and flirtatious manner...concealed ulterior motives.
>
> *(Murphy 2001, 95)*

FIGURE 2.5   Nuestra Señora de la Caridad del Cobre (author's souvenir collection)

Believed to have inherited her more refined qualities from her European heritage and her more visceral instincts from the African side, the Mulata potentially represents all Cuban women.

While it is popularly believed that the majority of Cuba's sex workers today are of African descent, statistics show that the majority are actually either white or *mestiza* (Fernández 1999). Nadine Fernández (1999) suggests that the confusion here evolves from the "strength of association between Afrocubanas and sex...[so that] sexual encounters between white Cubans and tourists seem invisible" (87). In other words, as Coco Fusco nicely summarizes, "Even though not all of today's *jineteras* are actually *mulata*...the [sexualized] stereotype still carries enormous power, so much so that to engage in sex work practically means to assume a *mulata* identity by association" (Fusco 1998, 155). While *jinetero* (masculine) literally translates as "jockey" or "rider" and describes street hustlers—who seek to fulfill tourist desires for meals, cigars, housing, or sex—the feminine form *jinetera* is often translated as "prostitute." I resist this translation, as there is little difference between *jineteras'* activities and those of Cuban men, especially white men, who follow the hustler lifestyle. In my view, *jineteras* are merely tapping into their most exchangeable form of **cultural capital**— dominant perceptions of their socially constructed sexuality (Bengelsdorf 1997; Fernández 1999; Fusco 1998; Gregory 2003; Kempadoo 2001).

Though theorists have begun to deconstruct the Mulata, very little has been written that considers Cuban masculinity as a racialized construct. In her dissertation, which considers interracial relationships in revolutionary Cuba, Nadine Fernández (1996) explains how young black men popularly termed *guapos* (tough guys) fit a longstanding Cuban (stereo)type of a ruffian street caricature that Cuba's premiere anthropologist, Fernando Ortíz (1906, 1986), long ago termed "*curros negros*"—black dogs.[4] In their tough-guy defiance and audacity, the so-called *guapos* constitute something of a hindrance to revolutionary ideology, but because they embody the ideals of "respectability and reputation," they also signify Cuban notions of masculinity (Rosendahl 1997, 64). Respect is earned by being strong and protecting one's honor (and that of one's broadly understood family), while reputation is earned by being sociable and sexually voracious—a contradiction that puts women's sexuality at the center of competition among men.

While the *guapo* stereotype was allowed some positive qualities—audacity, charm, virility—that are closely aligned with Cuban understandings of masculinity, other "masculine" qualities such as bravery, leadership, and articulateness were considered rare among Cubans of African descent and were reassigned to white Cuban maleness.[5] And even though *mestizaje* (racial mixture) was posited as the national ideal, *mulato* males were imagined to inherit the worst traits of both races—untrustworthiness, impotency, laziness—because of theories that race mixture begat "mongrelization" (de la Fuente 2001; R. Moore 1997; Young 1995). These tropes are revisited time and again on today's Cuban television, especially in dramatic *telenovelas* like "*Las Huérfanas de la Obra Pía*" and comedic variety shows like "*Pateando la Lata*.[6]"

Despite these racialized differences in understandings of masculinity, Cuban men remain united in their protective stance with regard to the women in their households. *Macho*, the root of **machismo** and *machista*, has come to mean biologically or "essentially" male.[7] In the same way that a male plant or animal is referred to as *macho*, so are human males. The corresponding female essence is called *hembra*. While the *macho* male essence may be encouraged and celebrated, *hembras* are socialized to become *señoritas* (ladies): chaste, proper, and respectable. *Machismo* is an exclusively male system that seeks to define femininity vis-à-vis competing masculinities:

[I]t was through the constant contest with other men over the bodies of women that they acquired the status of successful or unsuccessful manhood. If a white man's honor was invested in the sexual purity

of the women in his family—his mother, wife, sisters, and most particularly his daughters—his social esteem and position among the
male brotherhood was measured by the degree to which he could
undermine another's honor; that is, one's honor is increased to the
degree that of another is diminished.

(Bengelsdorf 1997, 242)

This kind of masculinist defense of honor has often been projected
onto Cuba's transnational relations, especially with regard to the United
States since the 1959 Triumph of the Revolution (Rosendahl 1997). That
is, if Fidel Castro and his *guerilleros* envisioned themselves to be defend-
ing the honor of Cuba, the past half-century of hostilities between the
two countries could be interpreted as a struggle in which the upstart
revolutionary *guapos* asserted their manhood in relation to the ultimate
in state power—"The Man," Uncle Sam. National imagery cast the revolutionary Cuban state as a man of color (more likely *mulato* than *negro*),
and the United States as a rich and powerful white man. Cuba became
the (female) pawn in this phallus-measuring competition. But in this
scenario the people of Cuba could not be imagined as *la mulata,* who
would have been open to sexual violation in a way that paralleled the era
of pre-revolutionary tourism (see Hodge 2001); instead, Cuba was portrayed graphically as a white (*rubia* or *trigueña*) woman (see Helg 1995;
see Figure 2.6).

Despite its pursuit of raceless and classless egalitarianism, the revolution's progress-oriented Marxian approach continues to link race and
nation. Through the evolutionist lens preferred by the Cuban elite (see
"The Meanings of Race" in chapter 1), the same late-nineteenth-century
cultural evolution model that located individuals on a sliding "cultural"
scale applies to nation-states as well. The "white" nations of Europe and
the United States predictably have "higher cultural levels," closely followed by the not-quite-white nations of Asia, while the "brown" nations
of Latin America and the Caribbean and the black nations of Africa are
lower on the spectrum. If the socialist revolution sought to "lighten" Cuba
through advances in the educational, medical, and social systems, then
one of the intolerable contradictions for many in Cuba's middle and upper
classes who ultimately fled into exile was that the revolution simultane-
ously required an economic "darkening" for them as class divisions were
significantly leveled.

The ethnographic data in the chapters that follow will clarify that the
race-gender-nation dynamic outlined here from Cuba's past are central
to understanding the segregation of Cubans and wealthy, foreign *yumas*
today.

FIGURE 2.6   Startled Uncle Sam looking at "Cuba" holding newborn "Cuban Revolutionist" (courtesy of Library of Congress)

Conclusion

That's why I don't think about the past. I just live in the present....And the future! And when I say I don't think about the past, I mean the past before 1959. Because before that, we were poor. And things were very different for us children than they are today. We went to school and we worked at home. We all knew how to clean the house, wash clothes, cook...everything! And because our mother had to work so hard, there was no questioning anything she said. If she said "Be here" we were there. It's not like today. These children nowadays don't understand. Like, I saw those twins today saying words so bad it was a shame. And young girls having children before they're 13 and 14 years old! That's why I watch over (*vigilo*) my 17-year-old daughter. Because if a young girl loses her virginity, her honor is ruined, and if she gets pregnant, her life is ruined....I talked to our doctor, and she referred to my daughter as "*señorita*." I said "*señorita*?" And the doctor said, "Yes, she's still a virgin." Virginity is rare these days and so that's why every day, I'm...*vigilando* 'cause you know how it is with young [black] girls these days.

—Barbara, age 64

Like Tía Caridad (whose narrative began this chapter), my neighbor Barbara reflected on *antes*—before the revolution. But while both of these women acknowledge how difficult life was before the revolution, Barbara diverges from Tía ever so slightly in her narrative. The first thing that Barbara does is draw attention to the distinction she makes between *antes de la revolución*—identified by the 1959 date of the revolution's triumph—and an unnamed *antes* that the rest of her narrative suggests may be the post-Soviet Special Period. Also, while Tía construes the prerevolutionary era in a wholly negative way, Barbara describes hardships in the past at the same time that she longs for the respect and morals of that time. Barbara's narrative highlights tensions across generations, while Tía does not mention any. Each woman provides insights into the many ways in which the past and the present, as well as race and gender, overlap and interplay with one another.

As Barbara (a dark-complexioned woman who would be described in Cuba as *negra*, or, more gently, *morena*) uttered the words "how it is with young girls today," she did not speak the bracketed word "black/*negra*," but subtly rubbed the inside of her left arm in a silent but visible Cuban discourse on race. Her audience of two other older women of color nodded their heads in recognition of the commentary she was making on the large numbers of dark-skinned girls engaged in *jineteando*. In today's era of revived tourism where women of color are capitalizing on their position as the objects of desire for foreign men, Barbara appeared to be expressing her displeasure that sexuality has (once again) become a key resource for social mobility among these women, whom Cuban racial and gender dynamics have historically fixed at the bottom of society.

In the chapters that follow, it will become clear that the revolution has not eradicated the meanings of race described in this chapter. On the contrary, according to Cubans' own racial criteria, their national identity is being "darkened" during the post-Soviet era in two distinct ways. First, the scarcity of the Special Period has led most citizens—regardless of skin color—into a "struggle" or *lucha* to survive that frequently involves legally and/or morally questionable activities associated with those "*de baja cultura*" (of a low cultural level). Second, Cubans are being treated as outsiders to the spaces of luxury and leisure offered to foreigners by the new tourism. In both ways, the post-Soviet context of socialist limitations amid capitalist excesses situates Cubans closer to the bottom of the global racial hierarchy than the revolution promised.

Notes

1. Avenida Simon Bolivar, popularly called Reina, is a main street in one of the poorer sections of Central Havana.

2. It has since been proposed that weapons that had been stored too close to the Maine's boiler-room became overheated and exploded; see "Remember the Maine" 1996. See also Helg 1995 and Pérez 1988.

3. Many members of Cuba's exile community continue to say with genuine fear that the revolution was going to "take their children" (see Garcia 1992).

4. In a personal communication (August 28, 2004), Fernández reiterated that the category *guapo* represents "a loaded nomenclature for people who don't really exist." I draw on the notion, however, because my interviews revealed that the type remains a meaningful one in contemporary Cuba.

5. See Helg 1995 on anthropologists trying to prove that Antonio Maceo's European heritage predominated over his African heritage in order to deem him a "truly superior man" (104–105).

6. The program titles translate as "The Orphans of Pious Works" and "Kicking the Can," respectively.

7. For more on the construction of machismo, see Ramírez 1999. My explanations of *guapería* and *machismo* depend on historically constructed, "traditional" ideals; nonetheless, such gendered categories derive their continued utility through the ways in which they have been embraced, shaped, and revisited by contemporary Cuban men and women. I do not intend to suggest that their meanings have remained static.

CHAPTER 3

Surviving through *La Lucha*

My former mother-in-law, Mami Teresa, is a devout revolutionary and *Fidelista* (Fidel supporter); she has a twin sister whom I call Tía Caridad. When Tía's old black-and-white Russian television finally expired, she and her adult daughter went without one for several months until their local Committee for Defense of the Revolution (CDR) deemed them destitute enough to be heavily subsidized in purchasing a new Panda color television from China. They would pay a very small amount, spread over an extended period of time, and in the meantime they would have a new television. Soon afterward, the news had spread all over Havana through informal networks that local CDRs would be distributing one or two televisions in this way to the neediest members of their community. Many began to mobilize to demonstrate that they were, indeed, among the neediest. Mami Teresa went into action too.

One day when I entered her house, Mami's 10-inch black-and-white television was missing from its stand at the foot of her bed. I began to ask her about it, but she urgently shushed me while she pointed to the square bundle wrapped and hidden in her closet. She whispered that she would go without in the daytime to back up her story that she had had to return the television she had borrowed years ago from her younger sister, Tía Angela. She would watch it only in the evenings with blankets covering the windows. Leading me to the dinner table in the front room, she and Tía Caridad had me read a letter they had written to the CDR chairperson to see if it sounded desperate enough. Mami then carried the letter around the corner to the CDR headquarters.

As the weeks passed, I heard updates on Mami's closest competition, described as a drunken retired amputee who did not participate in any "voluntary service" to the revolution as she did. When, at last, her CDR met to decide whether she or the amputee would get the first television to be distributed in their neighborhood, the committee chose the amputee. "¡*Esta es una mierda!*" (This is bullsh_t!), she exclaimed angrily; she would rather buy her own than take a handout from the group that had wronged her! I felt for her, but I also wanted to remind her that she was, in fact, trying to scam them.

But then it occurred to me to wonder, who was manipulating whom? My (then) boyfriend Yeshua, fruitlessly attempting to find a smaller, less expensive color television than the Panda brand his mother had hoped to wangle, complained, "You know how it is in a centralized system— the same three TV sets are everywhere, with the US$390 Panda costing the least." In Cuba's socialist system, I realized, the state, rather than the market, dictates the availability and cost of goods—so the state also needs to control demand. The Cuban government had likely spent a significant amount of cash on the Chinese televisions; now it had to persuade the people that they needed new TVs.

The majority of Cuban citizens earn peso salaries from the state that range from approximately CU$150/month (US$7) for manual laborers to CU$300/month (US$14) for professionals. Mona Rosendahl (1997) documents how most households can meet their basic needs using their monthly **ration books** or in state-subsidized stores that sell in Cuba's national currency (*Moneda nacional*, MN). Because everyone has access to such low-price peso goods as rice, potatoes, or coffee, they are often scarce. More durable items like underclothes and shoes that can only be purchased on the ration book once or twice a year are often of poor quality and undesirable. Since dollars were legalized in 1993, Cubans may also legally convert their MN into *pesos convertibles* (CUC) at a 22-to-1 exchange rate in order to buy on the (comparatively) free market goods like the Panda televisions that are often of foreign origin and higher quality. People carefully weigh cost against desire before pooling their pesos for conversion.

In order to offload the televisions in a nonadvertising society that frowns on materialism, the Cuban government would have to be creative. The apparent solution was to give the sets away to those determined to be most in need. Their marginally less needy neighbors, thus brought face-to-face with their own desire for a new color television, would then scrimp and save until they could eventually buy the colossus—which features a timer and programming for more than 100 channels, even though Cubans have access to only three.[1]

What does it mean when people who believe they are "good revolutionaries" game the system for personal gain—and the system games them back? What are the implications of such individualism for state authority? This chapter addresses these questions using the local trope of *la lucha* (struggle), a Cuban inflection of the global trend toward declining state power and rising individualism and materialism. The ways in which everyday people struggle to get by in today's Cuba involve the racialized

FIGURE 3.1   Cuban Family Color (photo by author)

concept of *cultura* described in the previous chapter. Specifically, the widespread illegal and immoral practices fostered by the dollarization of Cuba's socialist economy mimic the racialized stereotypes of *gente de baja cultura* (uncultured people). The contemporary economic hardships generate a constant need to hustle, scam, and creatively maneuver that "darkens" people in ways that go beyond skin color.

I use the term "everyday Cubans" to signify those who are often referred to by the Cuban government as "the masses" or "*la gente*" (the people). I use it primarily in contrast with "the Cuban government," though it is important to recognize that outside of their official capacities, members of Cuba's vanguard (Communist Party elite, presumed to have a higher political consciousness) also have to maneuver their way through day-to-day survival during the Special Period. It is even more important not to homogenize or flatten the diversity of experiences among Cuba's eleven million citizens, so this book provides ethnographic examples from throughout the island and from an array of ages and racial groups, and it highlights the racialized and gendered nature of Cuban society (see Figure 3.1). Everyday life is fundamentally linked to the raced and gendered processes evident in the touristic and global spheres.

La Lucha

> *Siempre hemos estado luchando. La historia nuestra es de lucha constante—lo mismo que en la manigua que en la ciudad. Pero ellos [los*

*EEUU] saben que con ese tipo de lucha—de guerra—no nos ganan,
entonces inventaron el bloqueo.*
(We have always been fighting. Our history is one of constant struggle—both in the countryside and in the city. But they [the United
States] know that they can't beat us in that kind of fight—of war—so
they invented the blockade.)

—*Hermina, age 26*

Cuba is a nice place to live—if you have money. We've got beaches
and all that, but if you don't have money…Cuba is a place with no
freedoms and you live through *la lucha*….

—*Juan Carlos, age 30*

As in many countries, daily life in today's Cuba requires a constant
struggle to survive. The difference presented by the Cuban context is the
historico-political meaning of the Spanish word *lucha*—a noun (or verb:
luchar) that means "struggle" or "fight." Whereas Hermina's use of the
term stresses historically continuous political and economic collective
processes, black market clothes vendor Juan Carlos uses the term in its
Special Period sense—as a way to acquire dollars by any means in the
name of the revolution.

The primary meaning of *la lucha* originates in the way the Cuban
government has defined "revolution." A socialist revolution, of course,
aims at ending social inequality by ending the economic exploitation that
makes the lives of the masses a constant struggle for survival. Socialism,
then, is the stage between capitalism and communism (see chapter 1,
"Socialism and Cuba's Revolutionary Ideal"). As Hermina suggests above,
revolution is understood to be a *process* rather than a one-time event: the
revolutionary process began during the nineteenth-century independence
movement, was thwarted by the U.S. intervention that concluded Cuba's
drawn-out war against its Spanish colonizer, and was rekindled when
Fidel Castro and his comrades overthrew Fulgencio Batista on January 1,
1959 (see the timeline at the end of this book). Since that time, the Cuban
people have been *luchando* (struggling) to fulfill their revolutionary goals
of building a politically and economically self-sufficient nation-state that
can provide for the basic needs of all of its citizens and support other, less
developed countries in doing the same.

Cubans are proud of the educational system developed under the revolution that has achieved near universal literacy in a free education system
from nursery school through university. Moreover, Cuba is best known for
its healthcare system, which provides free medical services to the entire
citizenry and exports medical professionals to developing countries to

provide free treatment. Though it is a developing country itself, it regularly ranks near the top in such key health indicators as child mortality and life expectancy. At the national level, then, the Cuban people have been quite successfully mobilized to *luchar* in the name of the revolution in a number of ways over the decades.

Since the Cuban government emphasizes this prolonged revolutionary struggle for survival at the national level, average citizens also feel encouraged to reveal their own never-ending struggle for personal survival. Thus in the post-Soviet Special Period everyday individuals have redefined the primary meaning of "struggle" for their own purposes, and hustling has (debatably) become a "revolutionary" act.

Transportation and Goods

As food and transportation became scant resources in the early 1990s—when oil and other imported goods dried up with the fall of the Soviet Union—they became the primary battlegrounds on which *la lucha* was carried out in everyday life. Long lines formed at neighborhood *bodegas* (ration stores) as women and household elders waited for hours on end. The kinship networks that had always been important to life in Cuba became crucial as families struggled to access scarce goods. The extreme rationing during the Special Period led Cubans to create a system for waiting in lines whereby one can be in more than one line at a time: Since others in line may be waiting in the shade or may have gone to shop elsewhere, one approaches a line and loudly asks, "¿[*Quién es el*] *Último* [*persona*]?" (Who is the last person?) That person is to speak up and tell the inquirer who is in front of them. With that done, one's space is marked and one is free to go about other business, returning to their space in line later (see Rosendahl 1997, 38).

I have been witness to—and the cause of—near melee on more than one occasion when this protocol was not followed. During one of my later research trips to Cuba, I decided to get a pizza at one of my favorite home restaurants near Havana's Capitolio building. I stood at the end of the short line and was waiting my turn when a woman approached and asked who the last person in line was. I responded. The woman in front of me whirled around and sternly corrected that *she* was the last person in line, also indicating who was in front of her. Realizing my mistake, I quickly defused the situation by stammering in Spanglish that I had forgotten to ask when I arrived. Once both of the women recognized my foreignness, they calmed down and returned to their places in line.

The *último* system is one of many ways Cubans have had to improvise during the Special Period in order to maximize available resources—time and social relations with family and friends—in the absence of available goods.

Moving the Masses

Another invention of the Special Period is what one interviewee referred to as the "*infáme camello*" (the infamous camel; see Figure 3.2).[2] The *camello* is a state-owned tractor-trailer converted into a bus with rises over the front and back wheels so that the shape is reminiscent of a camel.

Whereas city buses that operate locally cost $0.40 Moneda Nacional (MN, or national currency),[3] these contraptions are designed to hold nearly 300 people for $0.20 MN and carry masses of Havana's citizens from the city's distant suburbs to its center and back again. *Habaneros* joke that the *camello* is like the weekly televised Saturday night movie because it may have "adult language, sex, and violence." Merely boarding is dangerous, as people push and shove to get inside with little hope of finding a seat. Drivers often pull away with passengers dangling from the entryways.

In the course of my fieldwork, I rode on a *camello* only once, but I admit that once was plenty for me. Inside, as I narrowed myself and held onto an overhead bar for balance, I found myself captured by the dark blankness in people's eyes. I wondered if they had to leave their bodily selves to travel in such inhuman conditions, crammed like slaves on a slave ship. I remember grabbing my purse more closely to my body when a man behind me squatted down close to the floor. Everyone had told me what hotbeds of crime the *camellos* were. However, the man turned out to be ill—dizzy from the heat and the close quarters. Like any well-prepared foreigner, I had Pepto Bismol pills and a bottle of water in my possession, so I gave them to him. Everyone who saw nodded in approval and collective gratitude.

Camellos were one of the state's solutions to the scarcity of mass transportation after the fall of the socialist bloc. Like many services that are available for national currency, they are affordable for most people and are not designed to make money for the nation, but—as can be said of the

FIGURE **3.2**   *El Camello* (the Camel; author's postcard collection)

Special Period more generally—the conditions provided involve varying degrees of swallowing one's dignity.

La Botella

Surely the *botella*—literally, "the bottle," referring to hitchhiking[4]—has been around since before the Special Period, but the practice has likely become an art form only in these recent years of scarcity. If the *camello* is the mass-oriented solution to the transit shortage, the *botella* is a more individualized solution.

> And then, because the *camellos* made me faint [because] there were so many people that I couldn't get any air … I decided to always travel by *botella* and I learned the *botella* technique very well: "Might you do me the favor of moving me forward [on my journey]" without offending anyone, not even asking where they were going, simply "can you advance me?"
>
> —*Hermina, age 26*

Botelleras are most prevalent at major intersections or on long stretches of road. While men certainly hitchhike from time to time, adolescent girls in their school uniforms, mothers with children, and sexily clad young women predominate since a male driver will more likely stop for a woman in need of help (women drivers are a minority and they are less likely to stop for hitchhikers for reasons of safety). They may wait for a half hour in the hot sun in high heels for a ride (see Figure 3.3), but the *botelleras* always seem to win this *lucha* in the end.

Again, in the *botella*, Cubans creatively mobilize their resources: social relations—"the kindness of strangers"—time, and the female body. The practice can be time-consuming and uncomfortable, but most *botelleras* make the best of the bad situation, chatting and joking while they wait as well as once they have secured a ride. Swedish anthropologist Mona Rosendahl (1997) accurately captures the cultural context when she explains, "part of the concept of having cultura and being a good Cuban is being 'happy' or at least acting as if you are" (45).

Por la Izquierda (The Black Market)

One of the most damaging aspects of the Special Period is that even the most revolutionary Cubans have been forced to engage in illegal or unethical activities from time to time in order to survive. As central warehouses were emptied of goods after the fall of the Soviet Union, people had to get things they needed in more creative ways. Before the legalization of dollars in 1993, black marketeers sold items like meat, eggs, and soap—items that

FIGURE 3.3   *Cogiendo la Botella* (Carrying the bottle; photo courtesy of Henrik Normann)

were not available by other means—for exorbitant prices to those Cubans who had illegal access to dollars from their families overseas. Today, dollar stores have helped to stabilize prices on the black market, but many Cubans still make purchases *por la izquierda* (literally "from the left-hand side," that is, illegally).

A Cuban economist explained to me that there are two different forms of black markets: one in hard currency and the other in national currency. Within the former, scarce items like seafood, clothes, and construction materials will tend to cost more *por la izquierda* than they would if they could be obtained legally. In the latter, by contrast, items like toothpaste, soap, or underwear that are supposed to be available through the *libreta* (ration book) will cost less than if bought legally with hard currency in a dollar establishment.

The black market today is stocked primarily from three different sources: state warehouses, neighborhood ration stores known as *bodegas*, and state-run dollar stores. All three involve another Special Period phenomenon that became especially pervasive after the 1993 dollarization of the Cuban economy, the **búsqueda**—the practice of "searching" for a way to use one's regular peso-salaried job to earn dollars on the side by pilfering and reselling goods. One informant told me that many people would not accept a state job offer if there was no opportunity to *buscársela*.

An example of warehouse pilfering and the premium for scarce construction materials is the cement my boyfriend sought in order to make repairs to his crumbling house. Since the fall of the Soviet Union, many supplies had long been unavailable in legal stores, and cement had "gone missing" from the streets for more than two years. Scouring the black market, he had asked at every construction site he passed if there was a possibility of buying a few bags but was told the foreign businesses were too strict with their inventories to risk it. Finally, several months after Hurricane Michelle had hit the southern coast of the island in 2001, the *búsqueadores* were able to move cement out of the central warehouses and into the streets of Havana again—at US$20 a bag. Whether the national emergency had forced the state to go into the free market and purchase more cement, or whether it had been in the warehouses all along, cement magically reappeared.

Similarly, many rationed items supplied by the central warehouse to local bodegas, like coffee, "go missing" for long periods of time and eventually resurface in the street. During my fieldwork, I never asked many questions about where the people who knocked on my door selling eggs at US$0.10 or chicken quarters for MN$30 (US$1.50) got their goods. I was generally too excited to have my household needs met to ask probing questions that might scare the vendors away.

In dollar stores, the workers, usually young (white) women, would take aside small, unnoticeable quantities of goods—soap, toothpaste, cleaning rags, beauty supplies, sanitary items—and stash them with their personal belongings. Later, they would go door-to-door—or, more covertly, invite friends over—to sell the items for slightly less than in the store. This *búsqueda* is briefly illustrated in the world-renowned Cuban film *Fresa y Chocolate* (Gutiérrez Alea and Tabío 1995) when Nancy, supposedly a member of the *vigilancia* (the vigilant neighborhood CDR), sells another woman black-market items from her apartment.

Given the possibility of job loss, fines, or even imprisonment (depending on the gravity of the crime), *búsqueando* is risky, but it can be quite lucrative. As a more aggressive form of *la lucha*, it involves figuring out how to use one's official state job to fill a public need while maximizing one's own material benefit.

Jineteros (Hustlers)

I first met the pair that I call "Shorty" and "Tattoo" on one of my weekly trips out of the "Cuban world" into an Internet café for foreign tourists in Havana's upscale Vedado district. Out of the corner of my eye, I saw a sandy-blond 30-year-old white man motion to his buddy toward me. As I was about to enter, his 35-year-old black-haired friend, who stood no more than five feet tall, approached. Shorty asked me if I was from Jamaica, explaining that they had "found" a $500 Jamaican bill and wanted to know how much it was worth in U.S. currency. I told them I did not know but would look it up for them online after I had sent a few emails. They were waiting outside when I returned with the news that it was worth about US$8, but instead of being disappointed as I had expected, they eagerly asked if I knew any Jamaicans who would exchange it for them.

We struck up a conversation and I told them what I was studying. Shorty and Tattoo told me they considered themselves *luchadores*—people who struggled to make a living in the Special Period of the Revolution.[5] They had both recently come to Havana from Ciego de Ávila in the island's rural central region in hopes of harvesting some of the foreign tourists' dollars. They had had what others would consider "good jobs" with a joint venture firm (co-owned by the Cuban government and a foreign business interest) that paid their salaries in both national currency and dollars, but the *divisa* (hard currency) they were paid legally was not enough to keep them away from the lure of the big city. Now they occupied their time hanging around areas of high tourist volume, assisting tourists with their local needs for *casas particulares* (bed and breakfasts), **paladares** (restaurants run out of people's homes), or female companionship. Hustling was difficult work, but they could make more dollars that way than in most legal occupations.

As we chatted on our way to the Malecón, Shorty delicately told me that a lot of people were *mortificado* (mortified) to talk to foreigners because it was illegal. They, on the other hand, thought the law prohibiting Cubans who were not registered as tourism workers from speaking to foreigners was stupid.[6] Tattoo lifted his shirt and showed me the letters "USA" permanently printed in red, white, and blue just beneath his belly button. When I asked him why he had the tattoo, he said, "*porque me gusta*" (because I like it). He then pulled out of his wallet a **letter of invitation** to Paris that one of his "friends"—a former client—had prepared for him but that Cuban immigration had refused to honor, leaving him stuck in Cuba.

For his part, Shorty, who was independently studying English to communicate better with their clients, told me he actually liked Cuba but there were systemic problems that he did not like. For example, without a pre-university diploma, "a construction worker makes MN$150/month which at today's exchange rate of MN$27 equals US$1 is less than US$6/month!"[7]

He repeated what I had by then heard several times in my interviews and conversations with Cubans: "What good is such a low national currency salary when everything—non-*libreta* food, clothes, unavailable or hard-to-find medicines—is in *divisa*?" Even before the Special Period, it was difficult to live in Cuba on the ration book: "There was always the *libreta*, but it got harder after the Soviet Union fell. Back then, it was illegal to have dollars." When I asked if it was still the Special Period, or if things had improved, Tattoo responded, "It's better, but not much. Like if this is where we were in 1990," he indicated by pressing the tips of his index and middle fingers to one spot on the Malecón wall, "then this [about five centimeters up] is where we are now." He threw his open-palmed hand up and casually over his shoulder in a Cuban gesture that translates as "absolutely nothing" or "worthless." I asked them if tourism had played a role in the slight change in the country. Shorty answered, "Yes, it's helping the government, but it helps everyday people very little, unless they work in hotels, drive taxis, or have access to dollars somehow, because now everything is in dollars and most people only earn peso salaries."[8]

Shorty and Tattoo demonstrate the complexity behind identifying as *luchadores* that one hears from Cubans of all walks of life. While Shorty acknowledged his attachment to his homeland, he also recognized its economic shortcomings. Tattoo, with his dreams of Paris and the United States, reminded me of many others I met who fantasized about the world beyond Cuba, simply inverting the state-controlled media's portrayal of everything in Cuba as "good" and the capitalist world beyond as "bad." Neither imagined world is interpreted with much nuance. Yet the two were reflective enough about their nation's political and economic situation to try to maximize their own place in it, even if it meant leaving steady jobs for a less secure, illicit lifestyle. Despite regular police harassment for merely talking to foreigners, as well as the constant threat of deportation from Havana back to the countryside, young people continue to be attracted to hustling. Even more than other *luchadores*, *jineteros* and their female counterparts, *jineteras*, look beyond the Cuban context and into the recently welcomed global market for their fortune.

Jineteras: Hustlers or Whores?

From my very first visit to Cuba, I had a rather unexpected connection to studying prostitution. People who did not immediately recognize me as a foreigner assumed that I was around foreigners because I was a *jinetera*—a female hustler, or prostitute. When I told Cuban friends that waiters and hotel security guards seemed to be treating me badly, they carefully explained to me that many of the most popular prostitutes among Italian men were *prietas* (dark complexioned black women) who wore their hair in long braided extensions. "So because I'm black…," I tried to clarify with Sigmundo, my security guard friend. "¡*No, no, no, mi amor! El color no importa aquí.* Color doesn't matter here. It's that a lot of those girls are darker, like you, and wear their hair like yours…." So I found myself considering these women's day-to-day experiences with a keen and personal interest.

When I asked most Cuban men I interviewed what they thought about the *jineteras*, most of them looked at the ground, shrugged their shoulders, and said everyone had to do whatever they had to do to survive. But when I asked the same question to Javier, a deep-thinking Rastafarian, he led me to a nearby store window and pointed out what he told me was the primary cause of prostitution in Cuba today:

> Do you see those shoes there? That is the reason that Cuban women are selling their bodies—to get nice shoes like those. If they'd never seen them, they would not want them. But here, everyone wants to look pretty. And they see them in the stores, in the movies, and on the feet of foreign women and prostitutes. So they want them too. But Cubans can't afford nice things like that in national currency; they have to sell their bodies to foreign men. It's a lack of *conciencia*, that's what it is. They put a price tag on their own worth and sell themselves to foreigners because they have no [revolutionary] consciousness.
>
> —*Javier, age 32*

Interestingly, Javier's street-level explanation is not far from what Cuban academics and policymakers argue: that these women sell their bodies because they lack *conciencia*, a word that translates as both conscience and political consciousness. They often add, however, that these conscienceless women just like having sex (see Bazuin 1997)—an explanation that is dangerously akin to the racial stereotypes from Cuba's colonial era that considered black, and especially *mulata*, women to be amoral sexual predators (see Figure 3.4). Indeed, the desire to restrict and otherwise label women's sexuality is a common feature of many nationalist movements, even ostensibly radical reformulations of personhood and citizenship like Rasta (Enloe 1990; Foucault 1978; Stoler 1995; Ulysse 2007; Wallace 1979).

Significantly, none of the women I talked to called herself a prostitute or even a *jinetera*. Rather, they simply called themselves *luchadoras*. But there was a significant difference by race. The five young black or *mulata* women I spoke with confessed that their need for dollars to support their

FIGURE 3.4   "FotoArt Cuba - Yoandra" (author's postcard collection)

families made them do "*cosas malas*" (bad things). The one white woman I spoke to, whom I had met as she accompanied two Israeli sex-seekers that I interviewed, rejected any association with what she called *putas* (whores). If she wanted to hang out with a guy, go to nightclubs, and eat at nice restaurants that she normally could not afford, why should she not? She did not believe that his giving her a few dollars at the end of the night to help her along her way made her a sex worker.

Just as Nadine Fernández (1999) found in her study of the relationship between race, class, and gender among *jineteras*, this young woman had rationalized her relationships with foreign men in a way that was not terribly distinct from what many women in the capitalist West recognize as dating. And she found the same distinction in others' perceptions of women: while white women were often conceived to be "dating" foreign men, black women who associated with foreign men—because of their visibility and the sexualized stereotypes of them—were understood to be *jineteras*. In short, even though the majority of the Cuban population has been forced by the difficult economic conditions of the post-Soviet Special Period to *luchar* in some form or another, when women of color mobilize the few resources to which they have ready access—their time and their bodies—their practices are disproportionately stigmatized (see Hodge

2001 on male sex workers called *pingueros*). Indeed, *jineteras* render visible many of the fundamental fictions about race and gender equality in Cuba. For their part, the foreign men with whom I spoke tended to perceive all Cuban women as sexually available to them, thereby mulaticizing the women in the Cuban racial terms described in the previous chapter (see Fusco 1998).[9]

Marrying the Other

> Oh, but it'll cost you! You've got to pay to be free! Yeah, I'm about love too, but right now....I want my freedom! I gotta get outta here.
>
> —*Yanni, age 29*

I met Yanni in April 2002, a little more than one month before Yeshua and I were married. As a black Cuban man who had married an African American woman eight months earlier (but was still waiting for permission to emigrate to the United States), he gave me advice on the international marriage process. Though there was relaxed laughter as I exclaimed my surprise at the $775 price-tag for the international marriage license, his response (preceding) had a bittersweet tone. Yanni's desire to leave Cuba seemed to overshadow his love for his pregnant wife, and neither could find fulfillment without large sums of money. Because the foreign tourist "has got to pay," the Cuban government has effectively turned transnational marriages into another Special Period commodity. Without questioning love as the basis of any marriage, this section considers transnational marriage as a form of *lucha* in which race, nation, gender, and capital feature prominently (see Brennan 2008; also Fernández 2010).

Security and Mobility

Mia was dressed in zebra-striped hot pants and a dark crushed-velvet tank top the night I met her at a mutual friend's home in Matanzas. Wearing her braided extensions up in a ponytail that displayed her large gold necklace and earrings, the 30-year-old bore an uncanny resemblance to the hip-hop artist Mary J. Blige. She had met Franco, her 48-year-old Italian husband of seven years, when she was a dancer at the Tropicana cabaret in Matanzas; she now spent most of her time in her recently renovated home with family or friends and talked to Franco on the telephone once a week. While the two had traveled together to Argentina and other places, he had never provided the letter of invitation required for her to go to Italy. He rationalized that since he worked so much when he was in Milan, it was better that she remain in Cuba with her family and friends. He usually returned to Cuba every month or two and stayed for about a month, but this time he had been gone for eight months. Mia was visibly anxious the night I met her because he would be arriving the next day. She could barely contain herself in anticipation of seeing her husband again. The two did not emerge from their home the rest of the weekend for me to observe them myself, but according to the local women's grapevine, Mia and Franco were deeply in love.

In my own neighborhood, the 35-year-old *rubia* (blonde) who lived next door to me, Conni, was also married to an older man who lived most of the time in Italy, as did she. Indeed, when I moved into the house, I initially thought the residence to my left was vacant. Within weeks, however, Conni had returned from Naples and begun a renovation project on her single-level Mediterranean-style house that involved new ironwork and bright yellow paint on her exterior walls.

Both Mia and Conni lived in homes that were enviable even by the standards of their professional-class neighborhoods. To judge from what I heard or observed, their lives and those of their close relatives are much more comfortable than before their transnational marriages. Still, despite the stories I heard on the street about women keeping their old Cuban boyfriends while marrying older, unattractive but wealthy foreign men, none of the neighborhood gossips ever intimated that either Conni's or Mia's marriage was based in anything but love.

Masculinity and Money

In contrast to these women with absentee older white husbands were Yeshua and Yanni, both *negros* in their late twenties married to black American women in their thirties. Yanni's wife, Valerie, had first traveled to Cuba with Pastors for Peace, the blockade-breaking group whose humanitarian mission is to bring needed supplies for the Cuban people. Months after meeting Yanni in Havana's Parque Central (Central Park), I brought pictures of his newborn daughter to him. Valerie had sent them to me from Los Angeles (where she worked as a telemarketer) while I was home preparing for my own Cuban wedding. If Mia and Conni lived in beautiful homes, Yanni's—like Yeshua's—showed few signs of a foreign spouse beyond his relatively nice clothes and the stereo he turned on full blast when we entered his home. He lived in a *solar*, the Havana equivalent of a U.S. housing project. My fieldnotes describe the humble conditions of his home:

> An old man sat silently near Yanni's door in the building's open-air central courtyard. There was also a big colorful rooster tied to a stake not far from the unlocked door that Yanni opened as his own.

He ushered me to a long tan couch covered by a crochet[ed] throw. There were two easy chairs facing an old large television set on top of which was the boom box. A single bed and a chest of drawers were across the room. To the back of the room an open bible lay on a card table.

Yeshua lived in what Cubans call an apartment, one of a lengthwise row of small one-bedroom residences fitted into the alley between two larger houses. Early in our relationship, Yeshua explicitly told me not to send money to him, though I was permitted to send it to his mother: "I am a man, and I can survive through *la lucha*." On the other hand, years later, after we had married, I once asked if he needed me to send anything, to which he responded: "Come on, Kaifa! You see how we live...." I took his male sensitivity too literally, while he never really believed that an American could be as chronically strapped as I was. The images of the United States to which he had access did not mesh with my life as a member of America's black middle-class, which continues to struggle with economic inequalities based in past discrimination. Yeshua and I managed the strain well enough when I was in the country; I knew it was important for him to "be the man" in the relationship even if I was the financial source.

Gina is a *santera*, a priest of Obatalá whom I met when we both were returning to Cuba through Cancun. Two years before, this 47-year-old white American woman had traveled from Los Angeles to Matanzas to undergo a rite in the African-based religion known as Santería. During that first visit, she had fallen in love with the 38-year-old son of the priest who conducted the ritual, and they had gotten married some six months before Gina's and my chance meeting. After a honeymoon at the tourist enclave of Varadero, where she was pleasantly surprised at the way she and Roberto (a dark complexioned *negro*) were treated by the staff, they settled in Matanzas because of her perception that interracial couples met with less racism in Cuba than in the United States.

Because Roberto's family is central to Matanzas's powerful Santería community, *la Religión* (as it is called by its practitioners) is central to their relationship. At nearly any hour of the day, one can find their spiritual godchildren or other community members at their home: consulting with the Orishas—the Yoruba deities—or socializing over cold beers or warm rum, or helping with the cooking and cleaning. Roberto's state salary is paid through a local cultural organization; the source of their comfortable lifestyle is the investments Gina had made as a corporate executive in California. She often talked to me about the difficulty of balancing the masculinist desire to be the breadwinner with the reality that one's foreign wife held the purse strings. Perhaps because she had more capital at her disposal than I did given her profession, age, or race—but more likely because she had a truly joyful and generous spirit—Gina proved more skilled at managing the balance than I did.

Race, Nation, and the Pursuit of Romance

On the eve of Valentine's Day 2002, Yeshua and I went to Club Palmera in Havana City. After dancing for a while, we went to the bar. Somehow Yeshua knew we were going to have problems as soon as the bartender quoted the Cuban price for the daiquiri I ordered: "I'm just worried the drinks will take so long and be so bad, they won't be worth it." He was right; when my drink had not arrived after about forty minutes, he tried and failed to get any of the three bartenders to change my order to a simple bottle of water. When I began to flag down a nearby bartender myself, intending to speak in American English, Yeshua patted my arm down, unwilling to depend on my status as a foreigner for ordinary respect. Eventually he walked up to the bar himself and returned with a bottle, but it turned out to have been opened and refilled with tap water. This time, Yeshua and the bartender nearly came to blows: "Look, it's fine for me to drink water out of the tap, but my girlfriend...." Before he finished the sentence that would have clarified my nationality, Yeshua stood up. The move made the bartender nervous: "*¡Qué pinga!* [What the f_ck?]" Yeshua defused the situation by asking, as calmly as he could, for a bottle of water that had not been opened.

Both "race" and our skin colors felt central to me that evening—even if our "Cubanness" was our "race." Each of us knew from previous experiences at Club Palmera that if my skin color had not masked my *yuma* status, we undoubtedly would have gotten good and quick service. I could not help contrasting Yeshua's and my experiences with Gina's and Roberto's experiences in the dollar world. All doors were open to them with minimal effort. But I had to continually pull out my passport, speak in English, or otherwise perform my foreignness because my blackness had overshadowed it. That night, Yeshua did not want me to play that emasculating role; he wanted to be any man with his woman. He wanted to protect his masculinity by standing up for us. And the result was almost violent.

Money has long played a role for both men and women in love relationships across cultures: In many Asian societies, families offer the woman's estate to the fiancé in the form of a dowry in order to establish a new household, whereas men in many African societies must pay a bride price to the woman's family in exchange for the loss of her labor to the household. Likewise, in many Western societies, including our own, men traditionally have bought their intended spouse a diamond engagement ring—the cost of which ideally corresponds to a percentage of his annual salary. The converse is also true: marriages frequently dissolve because one partner (often the male) does not earn enough money, or because the other partner earns too much (generally the female). Similar processes were features of colonial Cuban society as well (see "Cuban Meanings of Marriage" in chapter 2). But today, the transnational context of international tourism side-by-side with the post-Soviet *lucha* to survive creates questions between parties about whether love is "true" or financially motivated.

> In the 1950s, back in our parents' day, everything was normal, there was true love and there was true respect. But now, we have evolved.... In those days, when a couple fell in love, it was completely real, there was not a question of whether they were ***interesados*** [financially motivated]. So now what happens...? Cubans, well, we like to look good, we like to dress nicely. For example, if you fall in love with a young lady, but you don't have a lot of money, well, she's not going to accept you because women want a gold bracelet, a gold necklace, a dress, nice shoes—they want to be fashionable, so, that is what's happening now. It isn't that practically every Cuban man is attracted to foreign women or that Cuban women are attracted to foreign men, but rather the people mostly want to have a better life. For example, if you have a daughter, you want her to marry a doctor....Everyone wants their child to be with someone better, for the better life they can offer.
>
> —*Malawi, age 30*

Like other cultural constructs, love and marriage practices appear natural to members of the group. Here, Malawi nonchalantly explained the Cuban expectation that social climbing is involved in love relations. Western tourists, on the other hand, are not as comfortable unmasking the commoditized aspects of interpersonal relationships. The most determined *luchadores* recognize this discomfort and hide their ulterior motives. Others, like Juan Carlos, take a calculated risk and make a straightforward proposition: "Kaifa, I would do anything—pay you, whatever you need—to get me out of this country. Just get me out of Cuba, please!" In either situation, these *interesados* darken not only themselves but also the reputation of *all* transnational relationships between Cubans and foreigners, whether there is "true love" or not.

Conclusion

> I finally get home—I won't tell you about the *camello* ride—and I keep living my life knowing that this is almost everybody's experience. This is life, what else could it be? I'm not aware every hour what's going on with the U.S. government or the Cuban government. I'm only aware of the goods that are missing in my life and my actions to get them. After all, even if the conditions were perfect in Cuba, my reality wouldn't change that much. There's always something to fight for day after day.
>
> —*Yeshua, age 24*

During an eventful daytrip to the beach, Hermina once told me she thought the many day-to-day difficulties "prepare Cubans for life." I have since wondered whether the life for which Cubans are being prepared is in fact a life where the state is no longer the caretaker. Rather than rely exclusively on a centralized state that doles out the goods and services that it contends its citizens require, Cubans are now finding individual solutions to their problems, like *la botella*, *la búsqueda*, and *jineteando*. The trends described in this chapter may suggest, then, that some of the neoliberal capitalist global processes that are diminishing the abilities of nation-states around the world to provide for their citizens are also insinuating themselves into Cuba (Huntington 1996; Ohmae 1995). Nonetheless, at least for the moment, these individualistic strategies continue to be mobilized in the name of such collective ideals as "the family" or even Cuban nationalism. Indeed, more than a few hustlers I spoke with joked that *jineteras* were "saving the revolution" with the dollars they attract to the country.

At the same time that the state seems to be losing its centrist hold on power, the widespread relaxation of the revolution's moral code constitutes a backward step in the longstanding Cuban quest for *cultura*. Although the revolution does not use the social Darwinist discourse of the early twentieth century (see chapter 1), Marxist-Leninism clearly defines "progress" in relation to Western cultural values. Like many other revolutionary objectives, socialism's promise of social, economic, and technological advancement aligned with the prerevolutionary Cuban aspirations to be a "cultured" people (see Pérez 1999). Yet, in Cuba, this notion of "culture" continues to be measured in racial terms that link blackness to a lack of culture or an absence of Western progress, and whiteness to Western cultural advancements. This understanding of socially acceptable behavior and stratification forms the backdrop to the everyday experiences described here. In daily interactions among Cubans, these racial meanings merely reveal themselves through the cracks; the following chapter elucidates how magnified they are when wealthy foreign tourists are incorporated within the context of Special Period Cuba.

Notes

1. Many households jury-rig antennas to receive network television from Miami when the weather permits; others creatively tap into area hotel cable satellites.
2. The *camellos* were decommissioned in 2007. See web-based story at http://www.cubanet.org/CNews/y07/jun07/19a5.htm. They have been replaced by extra-long buses from China that have large airy windows and piped-in music.
3. In Fall 2001, with an exchange rate of MN$20 = US$1, MN$1 was equivalent to US$0.05. As of my last visit in July 2008, the exchange rate was MN$22 = US$1, and MN$1 was equivalent to US$.045. During my long-term research in 2001–2002, the exchange rate fluctuated from a high of MN$18 = US$1 in August 2001 to a low of MN$25 = US$1 in spring 2002 (after the terrorist attacks of September 11, 2001, which affected tourist travel worldwide).
4. When hitchhiking, one points the thumb upward while the rest of the fingers curve inward, so it looks like one is holding a bottle.
5. In references to occupation, *luchador* is used as a euphemism for hustler or *jinetero.*
6. I have found no law stating that Cubans cannot associate with tourists; rather, as is the case with Cubans entering hotels, gatekeepers and authorities so forcefully discourage such interactions that they have essentially institutionalized fear among the populace.
7. While Shorty told the story to emphasize the relatively low salary construction workers receive, as described previously the Cuban salary scale is relatively egalitarian. It should also be noted that the low national currency salaries are misleading when converted to dollars because the conversion presumes expenditures will also be in dollars, which is not necessarily a valid assumption.
8. This interview was conducted in 2001. In 2004, Fidel Castro officially declared the crisis of the Special Period over because the Cuban economy had so greatly improved. Nonetheless, the "Special Period" concept remains relevant because the hard currency generated by the revamped tourism industry and the legalization of U.S. dollars in 1993—capitalist tools, repugnant to Soviet-era socialism—feature significantly in overcoming the national crisis.
9. For male sex tourists, skin color was primarily a matter of their own tastes as well as cost. Whiter skinned women can charge more, though tourists' tastes vary widely by nationality.

CHAPTER 4

Tourism and Belonging

I once asked Yeshua why Cubans were not allowed in hotels: was the practice really about preventing prostitution (as the official explanation claims), or did the government not want struggling Cubans to see the capitalist materialism in which tourists luxuriate, as my research had begun to suggest? Yeshua preferred the *jinetero* explanation:

> [A] random Cuban can't pay for a room at $60–$70.... And if they do have the money—there's something dark about that money because it's not possible if you are a Cuban, living in Cuba, working like a Cuban that you can make that kind of money. Most of those cases have to do with prostitution. Because they [that is, the government] want a really, I might call it, healthy tourism. They want their tourists to meet... "the real Cuban people," not prostitutes[1]....
>
> —*Yeshua, age 24*

I pressed him on his answer because it seemed to me discriminatory that all Cubans were being prohibited from interacting with tourists when it was only a very small percentage of the general population—the *jineteros*—who were the problem. Rather than counter that similar policies are employed elsewhere in the Caribbean, Yeshua argued that exclusion was valid to protect the image of the revolution abroad: "Can't you see," he shouted, "that the only way to fight that [exportation of negative images] is to prohibit [all Cubans]. No Cubans! No Cubans! *No Cubans!*... They [the government] don't care if we look like we're discriminating [against] our own Cubans," he concluded. I was alarmed by language that resonated of U.S. or South African enforced racial segregation; it felt inconsistent to me that such language was being used in the name of a revolution that purportedly sought to create an egalitarian Cuba. The apparent contradiction was resolved only when I began to unpack the nature of the relationships among tourism, race, and belonging in today's Cuba.

The Cuba experienced by tourists is markedly different from the Cuba of Cubans. In addition to the sense of **Otherness** and difference that tourists so frequently seek when they travel (Bruner 2005; MacCannell 1976), Cuba's dual economy—which permits one lifestyle for those with access to hard currency and another for those who have mostly pesos—also distinguishes the two experiential worlds. Mass international tourism (the form that predominates in Cuba and is preferred by the government involving large numbers of resort tourists) is a capitalist business that requires prompt, smiling service and systemic efficiency. Cuba is a socialist country in which efficiency is rare because of the centralized system of economic organization, and in which one might hope for "promptness," "smiles," or "service" but seldom all three at once. While their Cuban hosts live constrained by the scarcities of the socialist system during the Special Period, tourists in Cuba generally exist in a leisure world of excesses—too much food, too much drink, too much time—though, by Cuban standards, they are charged exorbitant prices for such capitalistic indulgences.

Because I was often mistaken for Cuban, I had both experiences: paying in *divisa* and having the sensation that "all doors were open to me" and paying in Cuban national currency—certainly a significantly cheaper mode—but sensing that I was an unwelcome interloper who therefore deserved second-rate services in such venues as hotels, nightclubs, and transportation. This chapter shows that (1) the Cuba of tourists is one of leisure and privilege, and (2) interactions between tourists and Cubans revolve around questions of power and belonging. Each of these attributes resonates with Cuban racial understandings about the status and place of whites and blacks.

In the word *yuma*, Cuban popular parlance captures the racial meanings behind both the status measures (*nivel cultural*) and the visual cues involved in Cuban tourism. The term (from Yuma, Arizona[2]) originated in the early 1990s and referred specifically to U.S. Americans (then rare in Cuba). *Yuma* now refers more generally to non-Cuban "Others," who, my interviewees repeatedly told me, were easily recognizable by their clothes (especially their shoes), their hairstyles or (for men) facial hair, their skin colors (especially obvious attempts at tanning; see Figure 4.1), and their entire *forma de ser* (their way of being). Because the majority of tourists came from Canada and Europe—especially Spain, France, Germany, and Italy—*yumas* were expected to be white. Nonwhite *yumas* who traveled to Cuba from elsewhere in the Americas often had their foreignness scrutinized through a **performative** lens that closely considered such cultural markers as clothes and comportment. Only after those behavioral cues had been accurately interpreted were black and brown tourists recognized and

FIGURE **4.1**   Sunbathing *yumas* (photo by author)

treated as *yumas* in a way that paralleled the cultural whitening described in chapter 2. Tellingly, the monied "race" of *yumas* was distinguished from foreigners from developing countries who were in Cuba to benefit from its international socialist outreach programs in medicine and education. Russian teens, for example, though often phenotypically *rubios* (blondes), were quickly dismissed as potential clients by hustlers with such comments as "they're just Chernobyl victims here for medical treatment." Visibly outsiders, but also easily recognized as nonmonied, this intermediate group might be "raced" *mulato*. For their part, Cubans were continually treated by tourism's gatekeepers as criminally as well as culturally suspect, paralleling what I have described as Cuban understandings of *negros*.

Who Tours Cuba?

Table 4.1 summarizes the statistics on the origins of foreign tourists in Cuba. While the U.S. government continues to limit the number of Americans traveling to Cuba without a license from the U.S. Treasury Department, U.S. Americans do travel to Cuba illegally through third countries, especially the Bahamas, Canada, Jamaica, and Mexico. Much more common, however, are Canadians, often on economical all-inclusive group-oriented resort tours.

Whereas the northern Europeans (British, Germans, French) share many parallels with Canadians, the Spanish share a linguistic heritage with Cubans and are less likely to isolate themselves in tourist resort areas, but instead stay in more expensive hotels closer to the cities, eating outside the hotel and experiencing the nightlife. Many middle-aged couples travel together, but there are also significant numbers of single Spanish men who meet and often marry Cuban women.

Italians may not be the most numerous foreign tourists, but they are certainly the most visible. The fashion and style preferences of *jineteros* follow Italian trends, and Cubans who (think they) have the right look often try to "pass" for Italian. Italians frequent the beaches, though they may reside in the city—often in *casas particulares* (private houses)—closer to the "action." While Italian women occasionally come individually or with their spouses, Italian men are the most notorious sex tourists visiting Cuba. Mexico has the largest representation among Latin American tourists in Cuba.[3] While there are, again, a few instances of family tourism, there are even greater numbers of men traveling alone. Mexicans travel to Cuba year-round, though generally for short visits (long weekends to five days). Some stay in beach resorts, although—perhaps because the beaches so closely parallel what is available on the Caribbean coast of their own country—the majority vacation in the cities.

Privilege and Place

> Havana is set up just for you wealthy tourists; you need to go outside to see real poverty.
>
> —*Javier, age 32*

My tourist interviewees told me they came to Cuba with specific interests in revolution, the beaches, music and dance, "the women," and "the people" more generally. Despite this diversity, one thing that tourists have in common is that their spending power distinguishes them from Cubans in the eyes of the state, tourism institutions, and everyday Cubans engaged in *la lucha*. The centrality of privilege and place resonate in the following tourist perspectives on (a) space and spending power, (b) gendered, raced, and global power in sex tourism, and (c) belonging and the meaning of revolution.

Tourism Apartheid

Three Spaniards whom I met in Santiago-de-Cuba—Grace (age 28), Marta (age 25), and Marta's boyfriend, Juan (age 27)—had initially planned to visit a friend in Honduras, but found Cuba cheaper. Given their stated desire to "integrate and participate" with their Cuban hosts, it is not surprising that they were interested in the "political situation, Fidel, and all that has happened since the fall of the socialist bloc." Like many young

TABLE **4-1** Cuban Tourism Statistics: Visitors per country of origin

Country of origin	2003	2004	2005
Total	1,905,682	2,048,572	2,319,334
Canada	452,438	563,371	602,377
EUROPE			
England	120,866	161,189	199,399
Italy	177,627	178,570	169,317
Spain	127,666	146,236	194,103
Germany	157,721	143,644	124,527
France	144,548	119,868	107,518
Russia	12,610	17,457	20,711
Holland	29,451	32,983	37,818
Portugal	28,469	25,608	28,780
Poland	5,562	7,439	8,295
Switzerland	24,630	23,106	21,918
Belgium	24,318	22,007	20,813
Austria	18,739	17,403	16,222
Czech Republic	7,777	4,102	7,425
Denmark	6,327	7,975	9,163
Norway	6,062	6,076	6,962
TOTAL EUROPE	892,373	913,663	972,971
LATIN AMERICA			
Mexico	88,787	79,752	89,154
Argentina	13,929	23,460	24,922
Venezuela	15,228	86,258	185,157
Colombia	13,122	13,408	16,175
Chile	11,938	14,500	16,744
Brazil	8,802	9,216	15,836
Peru	5,704	6,072	6,225
TOTAL LATIN AMERICA	157,510	232,666	354,213
OTHER			
United States of America	84,529	49,856	37,233
China	4,811	7,007	8,700
Philippines	12,718	9,932	13,389
TOTAL OTHER	102,058	66,795	59,322

Source: (adapted from Office of National Statistics, Republic of Cuba)

2006	2007	2008
2,220,567	**2,152,221**	**2,348,340**
604,263	660,384	818,246
211,075	208,122	193,932
144,249	134,289	126,042
185,531	133,149	121,166
114,292	103,054	100,964
103,469	92,304	90,731
27,861	29,077	40,621
35,871	33,605	33,548
27,304	25,442	25,542
8,569	11,598	21,730
19,962	18,588	17,140
18,886	17,256	15,681
15,384	14,492	13,450
7,562	8,547	11,214
9,296	10,156	10,179
8,211	9,881	9,974
937,522	**849,560**	**831,914**
97,984	92,120	84,052
30,383	37,922	47,405
83,832	33,593	31,931
16,053	18,594	22,178
16,110	14,951	18,895
11,024	12,165	13,865
6,436	6,179	9,598
261,822	**215,524**	**227,924**
36,808	40,521	41,904
9,276	10,864	11,252
13,405	9,067	10,567
59,489	**60,452**	**63,723**

tourists with whom I spoke, the three were interested to see the status of the Cuban revolution, but they were not always excited about the reality they found. Grace expressed frustration with what she called "tourist ghettos":

> Here there's one Cuba for tourists and another Cuba for the Cubans. A Cuban can't freely hang out with a tourist because the police are going to mess with him. I was very upset about the segregation in my first few days here. When you grow accustomed to segregation as a tourist you feel like you're on a different level (*nivel*) [from the Cubans].
>
> —*Grace, age 28*

Later in her interview, however, she expressed annoyance that *jineteros* had received commissions of US$5 for leading them to *casas particulares* that they might not have found on their own.

These Spaniards' experience highlights the tension between tourists' desire to develop nonfinancial relationships with Cubans and the Cuban authorities' recognition that tourists symbolize foreign capital not only to the state but also among the general populace. At the same time that many tourists are attracted to the country by the hope of getting to know "real Cubans," others are repelled from repeat visits by hustling and theft that give the impression that all interpersonal relationships between Cubans and tourists are economically motivated. Only a small percentage of tourists venture beyond the *jinetero*-lined path laid out in their guidebooks to forge genuine relationships with members of the general Cuban populace, who are too busy with the *lucha* of their day-to-day lives to think about the foreigners in their midst more than in passing. Yet the Cuban value for sociality and hospitality, as well as genuine curiosity about other places and people, provides an opening for interactions with individuals who are not professional hustlers. I have sat in the living rooms of many friends and acquaintances who refused any payment for the food, drink, or medicine they had provided me, even in worker–client capacities.

Some resort tourists seek to minimize financially motivated interactions by paying the bulk of their expenses—airfare and all-inclusive hotel—in their home country. Ezekiel, a 23-year-old concierge at a hotel in Acapulco, Mexico, decided to take his vacation in Cuba for "no specific reason." All he wanted to do was luxuriate for a week in specialty Body Shop soaps and bath products he had brought with him. He decided he could best accomplish this in the US$180/night Havana Libre Hotel in the center of the capital city's trendy Vedado district.[4] When I met him in the travel agency in the hotel's basement, he was trying to relocate to a cheaper, US$55/night all-inclusive hotel because he was running low on cash. Unfortunately, he did not realize that American Express is not accepted in Cuba because of the U.S. economic embargo: "I don't understand why! Everything's in dollars anyway."

As I treated Ezekiel to dinner during our interview at the Bodeguito del Medio—the restaurant in Old Havana famous for inventing the *mojito* cocktail to suit Ernest Hemingway's palate—I also spoke with two of his countrymen, Siggy and Rubio, whom Ezekiel had met at the hotel not long before our chance meeting in the travel agency. The latter two, who had finished a road trip around the island the day before, explained what impressed them most about Cuba: "In Mexico it's a common sight to see people sleeping in doorways or children begging, while in Cuba it never happens. In Cuba, they treat foreigners like kings and they'll give you anything." Ezekiel thought the Cubans had an ulterior motive, so he switched to English to exclude the others as he explained, "The reason they're treated like kings here is because they've got money. You can tell they're from money, even in Mexico, just by the way they talk." I knew they spent freely—in three hours I had seen them run up a tab of US$90—but as I observed them interacting with their hosts I concluded that they also differed from most tourists in other ways.

For example, when we arrived at the restaurant at five o'clock PM, they greeted members of the waitstaff by name, having been there the previous night. They tipped the mariachi band heavily for letting our group sing our requested songs with them at the top of our lungs from atop the tables on which we had dined earlier. Moreover, when the restaurant closed six hours later and we finally had to leave at eleven o'clock PM, they were not angry when we could not find a cheap place to dance as I had promised. They were just as happy to sit outside near Havana Bay, where one flirted with a *trigueña* while the other talked politics with a fisherman. It seemed to me that Siggy and Rubio had located the delicate balance of genuinely being interested in their hosts and accepting the reality that, as foreign tourists who were members of their home country's (upper) middle class, they had money that those hosts wanted and needed (an issue that I revisit shortly).

Sexual Conquistadors

Like many men from Europe, and Italy especially, I had heard so much about…the girls. And it is likely because they have a difficult time meeting women in their own countries—that may be my own experience as well. But it's just such an alienating experience because really what everyone is looking for is a relationship. I have on occasion been with prostitutes in Europe and there, it can often be, at worst, brutal—with women wanting you to pretty much do your business and get it over with. [In Cuba] it can be much slower, with caresses and dinner and drinks....More romantic—and that's a nice change for me.

—*Giovanni, Italian tourist, age about 40*

During the second week of my preliminary field research, I met two young Israeli men—David (age 24) and Eli (age 23)—who were staying at the same *casa particular* as a British friend of mine. They had just returned to Havana after traveling the island in a rental car with the objective of sleeping with a different woman every night. When I glossed this as meaning that they were seeking prostitutes, David explained that that they had not paid for sex the entire trip: "If you consider anyone you buy a drink, spend time with—whether you sleep with her or not—and help with cab fare to be a prostitute, that's one thing. Then I guess they would be prostitutes, but I don't see it that way." Rather than seeking prostitutes, they told me they were seeking *chicas*—girls.

As David was indicating, sex tourism in Cuba (and many tourist destinations worldwide) can be divided into a continuum of types. At one extreme are prostitutes, the "ladies of the evening" who actively solicit sex for money. Given the revolution's objective of cleaning up prerevolutionary tourism's brothel image, such "streetwalkers" (men or women) are rather few in Cuba. I have also read on-line reports of "escort services" for much higher end clients that presume a cash-for-sex basis; again, the scale of such sex work appears to be relatively small. It is important to note that prostitution is not illegal in Cuba, though pimping is.

The center of the sex work continuum in today's Cuba is composed of *jineteras*. As I argue in chapter 3, these individuals are better conceived as hustlers than prostitutes. Although young girls (under the 15-year-old age of sexual consent) have also begun to hustle, many *jineteras* are well-educated professional workers in Cuba's peso-salary sector, who have the option of hustling regularly or only occasionally. While many initially may have been attracted to *jineteando* for economic reasons, some report enjoying the nightclubs, dinners, and clothing their foreign "boyfriends" have introduced to their world. Compared to their everyday lives, time spent with wealthy foreign men often constitutes a kind of waking fantasy.

With professional prostitutes at one end and *jineteras* in the middle, David and Eli's *chicas* round out the sex tourism continuum. These are average young women who may meet a foreigner at the beach, walking down the street, or talking with friends and who have the time and curiosity to engage in an adventure with a "new friend" for anywhere from a few hours to a few days. Money is not the motive, for in most cases the women are going about their own business when the opportunity arises; at the same time, the Cuban *lucha* is an ever-present reality. One looks out for her own interest to the extent that her personal values allow.

I asked David and Eli to show me around "their Havana" before they returned to Israel in a few days. Since my attempts to interview sex workers themselves were largely thwarted by raced and gendered expectations that I was a competitor for foreign male attention,[5] an evening with these men provided a lens on the practice of sex tourism. Our first stop was Club Palmera, a somewhat seedy club in Central Havana. The two men paid the US$5 cover charge for non-Cubans (Cubans paid $3) and we headed into the cabaret, where the ratio of women to men was 15 to 1. David and Eli identified most of the women present to be prostitutes, as opposed to the *chicas* they preferred.

David and I sat on one side of the booth while Eli sat on the other, leaving the seat by his side empty as a beacon. I watched countless women approach and ask him for a cigarette; one woman did a winding salsa step in front of him but he shook his head "no" and she moved on; a woman later plopped down in the seat next to him and demanded a cigarette; he lied and said he had no more. She would not budge. Since he was ignoring her, I took the opportunity to ask Eli (in English) his perception of Cuban women. He responded crassly, "They see us as nothing but white dicks with money!" But soon, an attractive young woman who was more his type walked by and asked him for a light to a cigarette she already had.[6] He gave it to her and shook his finger at the girl sitting next to him, signaling she was to get up as he pointed to the new girl that she was to take her place. He bought her a drink, and the two danced the night away to pounding Euro-techno music.

After leaving Club Palmera, the three of us ran into several men from the United States on the seaside Malecón. Given the brief (and perhaps unseemly) contexts in which I interacted with them, I differentiate the groups of men here much as a tourist would—not with pseudonyms, but by their approximate ages and their places of origin.

The first group, in Cuba to study drums, comprised three twenty-something-year-old American men and one from Holland. They expressed shock at the sexual exchanges occurring in today's Cuba: "I'm just waiting to meet one Cuban woman who's not selling her body or being sold by her brother" and "I didn't realize that people actually sharked—I mean, I'm from Holland and just don't get it."[7] The U.S. restrictions on travel to Cuba have apparently shielded much of the younger generation. While young people imagine Fidel Castro and Ché Guevara's revolution or Afro-Cuban drumming and religion, older generations of Americans are more likely to recall Cuba's prerevolutionary reputation for sex (see Schwartz 1997).

The second group of American men, whom we met at an open-air restaurant near the Capitolio that was filled with prostitutes, spoke in ways that were more contradictory and evasive. "Mr. Seattle" was very slick, and as we talked about his purpose in Cuba, he mentioned nothing about the prostitute I had seen him with—nor did I. The two middle-aged Southern men (from Florida and Kentucky) who bought me a drink (probably so that I would not judge them too harshly) said only that they were having a great time so far, with a smiling wink that indicated the beautiful escorts who stood beside them, waiting to be seated. As the police approached, "Mr. Kentucky's" lady-friend grew more anxious and told him that they needed to be seated. The man remained unrushed and continued talking to me, but I made it plain to him that "she's going to get fined or arrested, though she'll have no problem if you're sitting at a table with her by the time the police approach you." I sent the women off quickly to an empty table, while the Kentuckian said, "Oh well, I'd better run along; I don't want to get anyone in trouble here."

"Mr. Boston" was young—maybe 20—and I perceived him to be performing an urban street identity for the Cuban friends with whom he sat. He had originally come to study drumming and had been in Cuba six months so far; he told me he did not intend ever to return to the United States. He acknowledged his girlfriend only when I mentioned that he was neglecting her by talking to David, Eli, and me for so long. Pulling a box of fake Cohibas out of his shoulder bag, he clarified, "No, man, I'm training her to hustle these cigars to men!" If the other women in the café were prostitutes, this woman may have been a *chica* or a *jinetera*.

In his analysis of "imperial masculinity," Steven Gregory (2003) finds that more than sex itself, men's global engagement in sex tourism represents power and control over a racialized and sexualized Other. As my preceding conversations with sex tourists illustrate, "many men maintain a dual and contradictory evaluation of women's identity and agency: they are either demonized as 'whores,' who care only about money, or romanticized as sensual and devoted partners who can be controlled" (Gregory 2003, 350). Eli exemplifies the former, and Giovanni (the Italian whose narrative began this section) the latter. The young American's lament that he was "just waiting to meet one Cuban woman who's not selling her body" illustrates Gregory's suggestion that "male tourists want women to affirm their desirability as *essentially* men" (350). Nonetheless, as I argue later, the women who take part in sex tourism are also active agents who frequently seek to manipulate this "imperial masculinity" for their own ends. Through the interplay of sexuality, emotions, and desire, the global sex tourism industry represents a complicated power dynamic in a context loaded with racial and gender implications.

Power and Belonging

> People from other countries can come here [to Cuba], but Cubans can neither enter their hotel nor visit the other countries.
>
> —*Niyelis, age 19*

One of the central spaces where tourists and Cubans interact is the hotel. There are rules for who belongs, who does not, and who is contingently permitted on the premises.

Borders/Boundaries in Blue

Inside hotels worldwide, the employees are the first level of interaction many tourists have with the local population. At the two-star Poseidon hotel on the outskirts of Havana, this includes an army of *mulatas* and *mestizas* who work in reception, the telephone room, the gift shops, etc.; white and *mestizo* food service workers (male and female) and bartenders (male); a team of entertainers with a balanced racial and gender composition; and custodians (older men of any race) and housekeepers (women of any race and age).

The first level of interaction most Cubans encounter upon entering a Cuban hotel is the security guards, but from the tourist perspective they are generally innocuous. This cadre of highly visible men were dressed in long-sleeved sky-blue shirts, dark narrow neckties, and dark slacks. Armed with walkie-talkies, they stood at nearly every doorway on the lobby level. At least one also wandered poolside at all times. In the United States, these men would be considered black. They smiled frequently, and I found them extremely helpful in many ways—the *mulato*, Juan, gave me suggestions on how to negotiate my bags the first day while his duty shift placed him at the entrance of the Poseidon; later, when he was working the night shift at the pool, he told me exactly how I could get reservations for the show at the Hotel Nacional. Another, Nigel, a dark-complexioned English teacher turned tourism worker, told me to ask when I needed anything—including the *jinetero* drivers he hired for a friend and me instead of the high-priced government taxi drivers stationed outside the hotel (a transaction on which he covertly received a commission).

Despite how nice they were to me, the primary function of these security guards was to keep Cubans out. Their helpfulness to tourists most likely had interested motives, though it was also true that their jobs involved long, generally uneventful hours, so interacting with tourists was a welcome diversion. That some of them occasionally engaged in improprieties merely signifies the malleability, flexibility, and humanity of such cultural structures.[8]

Worker Invisibility

I was watching one of the Varadero hotel housekeeping staff—a black woman—mop the tiled floor of the open-air, poolside restaurant. While other hotel workers tried to walk around the wet paths she created, a tall, dark-haired *yuma* male walked directly across the floor as though the woman were not there working. With the exception of the Poseidon Hotel in suburban Havana, where for some reason the janitors, housekeepers, and security staff did not hesitate to interact with guests, in virtually all the other Cuban hotels I visited,[9] all but the entertainment staff seemed to blend into the background as they might in any other country. In the metaphor made famous by Ralph Ellison's *Invisible Man* (1947/1992), the maid was *supposed* to be invisible—and to most guests, essentially she was.

From the Cuban government's perspective, it may be that optimally, everyday Cubans should be invisible to the tourists, who should be wrapped up in hotel package deals. That may be the reason for the prohibitions against Cubans in hotels or even talking to tourists: the state would prefer that tourists outside their hotel confines interact with one another, while gazing at historic buildings and museums, rather than with the Cubans they may come across along the way. Those rare Cubans who seek to make themselves visible on their own terms—*luchadores* and other hustlers—counter that the revolution promised that Cuba was theirs and that they, too, belong. That is, *jineteros* challenge the state not only because they stray from tourism's script, but also because they do so in the name of socialism.

Of Bracelets and Belonging

One mark of belonging is the plastic hospital-style bracelets issued to tourists staying in all-inclusive hotel resorts throughout the country—most notably the beach areas of Havana's Playas del Este, Varadero, Trinidad, Cayo Largo, and Cayo Coco. Such bracelets are used in hotels and nightclubs around the world, but their meaning is magnified and somewhat distorted in the socialist yet racialized context of today's Cuba.

Upon checking in, each guest at an all-inclusive hotel is given a brightly colored bracelet and told that they should wear it at all times in order to use the hotel's amenities. Most guests keep their bracelets on far beyond the confines of the resort, but I met several who resented their "dog-tags" and refused to wear them at all, keeping them, instead, in pockets or purses. After a few days in the hotel, one is generally known to security and staff and would rarely be barred from the hotel's facilities even without a bracelet. Nonetheless, I witnessed a few incidents in which security officers asked to see guests' bracelets. If the bracelet were not produced, a key or valid room number would suffice. On very rare occasions, I saw security actively pursuing foreign white individuals who sought to use their color advantage in order to enjoy the hotel's amenities, though they were not actually guests.

Among the few Cubans who may partake in the luxuries of the new tourist industry are honeymooners and vanguard workers—the top producing, hardest working exemplars of the revolution's New Man ideal. Because the dollar prices of the hotels are generally far beyond what any Cuban who works for the state can afford, their visits are highly subsidized, and they are generally allowed to pay in national currency.[10] To signify what their peso rate allows them—the same all-inclusive meals as tourists, but limited alcoholic beverages—Cuban tourists wear differently colored bracelets. In my interviews, I never heard any Cubans complain about their differential tagging. Indeed, they were grateful for the opportunity to partake in resort tourism at all and acknowledged the arrangement as completely fair. The exception made for these exemplary Cubans lends credence to Yeshua's argument that Cubans are restricted from hotels in order to protect tourists from hustlers.

Cubans who are neither vanguard workers nor honeymooners are rarely permitted beyond the lobbies of hotels without paying a day-fare (or having it paid by a guest). The pass they receive for the US$5 to $10 fare allows them to eat, drink, and swim, but visiting Cubans are not allowed into guest rooms at all unless they are married to the foreigner whom they accompany. The high price of entry precludes harassment by hustlers, and if the gatekeeper is at all suspicious, he can always refuse service. Indeed, the very presence of security guards at the door serves to intimidate and remind the majority of bracelet-free Cubans that they must remain outside hotels altogether.

The *Yuma / Jinetero* Dynamic

What is the balance of power between tourists and Cubans? Might the reciprocal relationship through which each is allowed to be part of the other's world be conceived as somewhat symbiotic?

Being Yuma

Compared to Cubans, who live within a restricted world on peso incomes and rationed goods, *yumas* are recognized by their Cuban hosts as an economically privileged group. However, *yumas* generally do not realize that they are also perceived by their hosts as somewhat ignorant—uneducated in Cuban ways. Two entertainers who worked in Playa del Este slapped their knees in laughter when they talked of a Canadian guest who had left the hotel and returned moments later all banged up. They had asked him what happened and were told that a car had hit him while he was crossing the street. Apparently the Canadian was unaware that driver courtesy and "pedestrians have the right of way" are foreign concepts in Cuba. Cubans have to be extremely creative just to get by in their daily lives. From their perspective, *yumas* are too pampered in their home countries to know how to survive in the harsh streets of Havana.

Embodied Cubanness

I have described *yumas* as easily identifiable by their skin color and other physical markers, and also by behavior. When the eyes were not enough to determine the high-stakes question of whether an individual "belonged" among the Cubans or the *yumas*, Cubans used their ears: could the person speak Spanish? With what accent? Still, an unfamiliar accent might merely indicate that the individual was from a different part of the island.[11] I was constantly confounded when the next resort in the quest to identify "Cuban blood" was smell. Yeshua once told me of an encounter at a nightclub: he was speaking French with a Haitian-born Canadian and, when two *jineteras* approached, decided to pretend that he was also foreign. The women suspected one of their countrymen was at the table and began to sniff them both. "*Eso, eso es Cubano*! (This one is Cuban!)," definitively exclaimed the one who had sniffed Yeshua.

I was sniffed on numerous occasions and was always found to be a *yuma*. I asked Juan Carlos what smell had to do with anything. "I don't know, I think it's something in your clothes, like what you wash them in, but you all don't smell the same as Cubans." I protested that I washed my clothes in Cuban detergent and bathed with Cuban soaps. Late in my research year, I asked Yeshua if I still smelled like a *yuma*. He said not as much as I when I first arrived, but despite how "Cubanized" I had become, my *yuma* scent still clung to me.[12]

Most fascinating to me were Cuban attempts to identify Cubans who lived abroad. No matter how white-complexioned they were, no matter what idiom or accent they had picked up in their new country of residence, no matter how wealthy they had become, in every instance that I observed, Cubans always recognized their kins(wo)men eventually. One night, Yeshua and I sat in an open-air nightclub. At the next table two women were speaking in Spanish with an accent that was not Cuban. Yeshua and I debated their nationality for half an hour; I argued that they were both *yumas* while he argued that one of the women was Cuban. To end our stalemate, Yeshua finally turned and asked the woman in question where she was from: "I was born in Cuba but I have lived in Venezuela for the past fifteen years." Yeshua celebrated: "I always know my people! *Lleva en la sangre*—there's something in the blood."

Many people with whom I talked referred to this same "blood" as though, in addition to its scent, it carried the genes for dancing and sexual ability. People preferred such biological explanations to my arguments about socialization and constructed racial and sexual identities. Still, I do not have an explanation for how astute Cubans are at recognizing "their own" and "Others." What is clear is that distinguishing between the two has grown increasingly important in the context of Cuba's growing tourism industry. Being Cuban signifies understanding the *lucha* (struggle for survival), while being *yuma* signifies having access to money and a more leisurely way of life.

Jineteros' Duty

Struggling with his *yuma* identity, Alex, a tourist from my home university, wrote the following e-mail to his family in the United States about his early experiences with hustlers in Havana:

> 8/25 ... The hardest part about being here as a foreigner are the street hustlers, taxi drivers and others who constantly call out to tourists in the streets. Having been accosted several hundred times on the streets so far ("Hello, friend, where you from? ... Cigar? ... English, yes? ... Looking for a house? ... Have you had dinner? ... Where you from?"), it seems that *jineteros* come from a combination of three things: [First,] Cubans' natural friendliness ("we Cubans are sticky" is how someone put it); [second,] tourists' difficulties in locating basic services in a society that has no signs or yellow pages, and [third,] the incredible power of the dollar here. The tricky thing is that we Americans can't understand that hustling is often about both friendship and money at the same time. We want to know whether he likes us or wants our money, when the truth is that it's a mix of both.
>
> —*Email home from Alex, U.S. tourist, age 28*

Contrary to how it may feel to tourists themselves, the majority of Cubans pay very little attention to foreigners. As I was repeatedly told by those who saw themselves as the "good" Cubans, only a very small minority of the country's citizens—"*los malos*" (the bad ones)—are involved in hustling as a way of life.[13] However, because they situate themselves close to areas of tourist activity—hotels, craft markets, nightclubs—it can feel to *yumas* as though *jineteros* are omnipresent. Most tourists, therefore, welcome the dearth of hustlers when they travel outside of Havana and its provinces to less traveled parts of the country—"the real Cuba" of those who seek authenticity. Yet I have brought obvious foreigners—both black and white, toting their telltale cameras and water bottles—to neighborhoods in Central Havana never mentioned by tour books, and no one paid the slightest attention to any of us.

Who are these *malos*—these threats to tourism (Hodge 2001)? Compared to other developing countries, Cuba's black marketeers are notoriously harmless; a number of tourists I talked to cited Cuba's low crime rate as part of the draw to vacation in Cuba as opposed to other Latin American or Caribbean destinations. While two women have separately told me they each wandered through Havana's back streets alone and had their necklaces snatched, the majority of tourists I met were amazed by the (relative) honesty with which *jineteros* conducted their business. For example, one young man from Italy told me he gave his watch to a *jinetero* for repair; they were to meet the following day at a particular time to conclude the transaction. The tourist later worried whether the hustler would actually show up but was pleasantly surprised to meet the *jinetero* on time with the working watch. This was certainly a foolish risk to take in any country; nonetheless, many hustlers to whom I have spoken prided themselves on their reliability.

As Alex had learned, a "smart" *yuma*—one who is not (too) gullible, is respectful, and establishes straightforward expectations—has the opportunity to experience Cuba with a level of depth unknown to the average tourist. As for me, in order to interact with the many hustlers I met in the course of my research, after a few unpleasant experiences I established a personal policy in which I would tell them up front not to try to manipulate money out of me: "Don't hustle me (*no me jinetes*). I will give you anything you want or need if you just let me know, but if you hustle me I'm gone." Probably because developing relationships and getting along with others are so highly valued in Cuba (see Rosendahl 1997), the magic words to get rid of a hustler, "*no me moleste*" (don't bother me; see Stanley 2001) are extremely effective. Hannah Elinson (1999) found that many tourists who are able to establish strong interpersonal relationships with *jineteros* return to Cuba year after year.

Commodification or Empowerment?

These people have nothing. People who have no possessions have
only their bodies. Women's bodies are being commodified because
it is all they have....

—*David, Israeli tourist, age 24*

Following the fall of the Soviet Union, the economic and social scenario
in Cuba has led many professional women—doctors, lawyers, psycholo-
gists—to search for hard currency in the sex industry in order to feed themselves and their children. Is it sufficient, however, to conclude that these
women have simply exchanged their bodies for money as David claims?
His own previously described touristic quest for free (as in unpaid) sexual exchange suggests that money may not be the only motive for women
(and others) who interact with tourists. Rather, many Cuban women have
embraced the same sexualized and racialized fantasy they represent to
foreign men. For example, Hermina suggested that foreign men liked the
"innate" caring nature of Cuban women: "That's just the way we are. We
like to dress up. We are very *caliente* [hot, as in passionate]. We like to take
care of our men. I guess that's why so many *extranjeros* [foreign men] fall
in love with Cuban women. Maybe they aren't treated like that by women
in their countries." Moreover, women actively capitalize on this fantasy.
At age 26, Hermina holds a degree in psychology but ultimately decided
that working with tourists would provide a more promising future. Male
tourists are not the only active agents in Cuban sex tourism; *jineteras* are,
metaphorically, jockeys who whip the money they desire from their johns
(Hernández-Reguant 2002). In other words, Cuban women mobilize and
manipulate stereotypes for their own gain, thereby commodifying both
themselves and national imagery.

A strict Marxist interpretation of this kind of **commoditization** presumes that *jineteros'* primary desire is to obtain money. The difficult economic conditions of the Special Period make this an acceptable, if flat,
materialistic explanation. But the desire expressed through *jineterismo*
may also be desire for activity—a desire to participate in the global community that is creeping into Cuba, by going out dancing and to restaurants
that Cubans cannot afford on pesos. *Jineteras* want to have "fun" instead
of sitting in a hot apartment watching soap operas, the news, or variety
shows on television with their parents, grandparents, and younger siblings.
Once in the domain of tourism, these women have actively mobilized the
resources at their disposal—their raced and gendered sexuality—to get the
global capital that Cuban men also seek using their available resources
(Cabezas 1998; Fusco 1998).

Consider Cari, a blue-eyed *rubia* (blonde) whom I first met in the summer of 2000. At the time, I assumed her to be a worker at my Havana hotel, since she would participate with the rest of the entertainment team in encouraging the guests in their merrymaking. I later found out she was not officially employed there at all, but was essentially a gentrified hustler who was seeking tips from the men who found her salsa dance movements enticing.[14] When I met her again three years later, she had just returned from traveling in Europe for a year with one of the famed Tropicana night-club's international dance troupes. Whereas in the past she had allowed her wavy sun-damaged hair to move freely about her head and frequently wore miniskirts or snug-fitting jeans with blouses that revealed her mid-riff, now she was dressed in a sleek one-piece black bathing suit with a matching ankle-length sarong, wore expensive chic sunglasses, and had her hair smoothly pulled back in a chignon. As we talked by the pool at one of East Havana's beachfront hotels, I detected an Italian accent to her Spanish that led me to verify with a mutual friend that she was, indeed, Cuban.

Cari and I laughed at the irony of how she was frequently mistaken for European and allowed access to tourist locales in Cuba if she carried herself and spoke a certain way, while I was mistaken for Cuban and regu-larly challenged as inadmissible. As a *luchadora*, Cari had mobilized her available resources—her skill at dancing, foreign perceptions of her sexu-alized body, and her skin color—to upgrade her standard of living; as a member of the Tropicana troupe, she ultimately achieved upward mobility within the revolutionary system. The vast majority of *jineteras* have fewer resources available to them.

Toward Symbiosis?

One reflection that I consider further in chapter 5 is whether *jineteros* and *bisneros*—the entrepreneurs of Cuba's informal economy—might be best conceived as the precursors of a business class in a future capitalistic Cuba (Freeman 1997). In a more liberal context, the barriers to legal entrepre-neurship would be lessened and it would not be illegal for Cubans merely to interact with foreigners, so the darkening stigma of their work would be lessened.

Jineteando is one of the rare sectors in today's Cuba that recognize the importance of friendliness and customer service. The relationship between *yumas* and *jineteros*, which is presumed by the Cuban government and the country's many non-*jineteros* to be antagonistic, has the potential to be much more symbiotic. As Alex recognized, at the same time that *jineteros* need tourists, tourists need *jineteros*. Like Siggy and Rubio, tourists who actually use and get to know *jineteros* have the opportunity to shed some of their *yuma* skin as they learn about some of the realities of life in Cuba and willingly diffuse their consumer status among their new "friends." In this way, the uneven power relations that underlie touristic interactions are equalized somewhat, and a degree of belonging is shared bilaterally.

One of the key impediments to more open relations between Cubans and tourists, however, is the state. As is endemic to the tourism industry more broadly, the Cuban government invites tourists to "see the country" and "see the people," but would prefer to contain the interactions between hosts and guests (Cheong and Miller 2000; Cohen 1995; Smith and Brent 2001). Because the tourists have spending power, they are (perceived to be) constantly in danger that a member of the comparatively impoverished host population will seek access to that money, whether forcibly or more creatively—money that the state seeks to gain for itself. Since the state desires to attract more tourists, foreigners are seldom chastised for violating the borders; it is the local population that reaps the consequences (Alexander 1997; Gregory 2003; Kempadoo 2001).

Conclusion

Cubans live through *la lucha* in a constrained world that strives to remain socialist, while tourists live in capitalist leisure. In interactions between and within the two conceptual worlds, the key questions are, "Who has the power" and "Who belongs?" Whereas the tourism industry generally posits tourists as the only ones who have power, Cubans occasionally seek to exhibit their authority in the tourist interaction as well. Tourists may have the dollars, but workers (whose jobs are guaranteed by the state) occasionally use their positions to remind tourists that they are the portals to an enjoyable stay. Like the *búsqueadores* described in chapter 3, even security guards find ways to use their positions in the tourist industry for personal gain.

By contrast with lower end tourism, in the higher end tourist establishments in Varadero, workers seem to make a concerted effort not to exercise any of the authority they may hold over tourists. Although they occupy the most prestigious positions in the country—those with access to the most tips in a prime market—the Cuban government's tourism schools seem to have trained them to be invisible. In deeper contrast still are those Cubans who counter authority and seek to make themselves visible to tourists on their own terms. *Jineteros* and other *luchadores* seem to be challenging the government to uphold its revolutionary rhetoric: Cuba should belong to Cubans.

Certainly, the exclusion of Cubans from tourist spaces is problematic from a nationalist standpoint, but it also has racial implications. Skin color—blackness, brownness, or whiteness—is a key signifier of who does or does not belong in touristic spaces: the whiter the skin, the more likely one belongs; and likewise, the darker the skin, the less likely they belong. As one Haitian-American succinctly put it, "Cuba is the worst place in the world to be mistaken for Cuban." Still, more important than skin color to determining inclusion or exclusion is the paired unit of foreign citizenship and convertible currency. If a wealthy Cuban is not welcomed as a guest in a tourist establishment, neither is a foreigner from a developing country who has only national currency—regardless of either of their skin colors. Foreigners with capital who "look Cuban" receive close (and often unpleasant) scrutiny largely because their skin color has led them to be mistaken for Cuban, not because of their skin color per se. Because the construct of race in Cuba is also grounded strongly in issues of status and belonging, such individuals generally have the opportunity to "pass" conceptually from a black(ened) Cuban into a white(ned) *yuma*.

How does race connect with a nation's political and economic organization? Cuban understandings of color and class have parallels to other Latin American contexts, while other Caribbean (and Pacific) countries also rely on mass international tourism as the cornerstone for their economies. Still, tourism presents unique challenges to Cuba's socialist project. Chapter 5 considers what the juxtaposition of socialism and capitalism in the context of Cuban tourism can teach us about tourist–host interactions in other sites of mass international tourism.

Notes

1. This conversation was carried out in English.
2. Three individuals I questioned about the origin of the word "*yuma*" mentioned the 1957 Western film *3:10 to Yuma* (these interviews predated the 2007 remake by several years). Like all borrowed words, *yuma* is a gender-neutral term whose article (rather than final vowel) determines the gender; therefore, a male foreigner is *un/el yuma* while a female is *una/la yuma*. Follow-up research in July 2007 reveals the new slang to be *pepe* or *pepa*, terms that more closely link foreigners with a prostitute's john.
3. As of Cuba's 2008 Statistical Report (*Cuba en Cifras*), Argentina was the only other Latin American country to send significant numbers of tourists, followed by increasing numbers from Venezuela, likely owing to increased political and economic ties with Hugo Chavez's government. Only infrequently during my fieldwork did I meet Puerto Ricans or Dominicans.

4. Before the Cuban revolution the Havana Libre hotel was the world-renowned Havana Hilton. It is now jointly owned and managed by the Tryp Company of Spain.

5. As I noted in the previous chapter, I did conduct a handful of interviews with women who identified as *luchadoras*, but the distrust was so palpable that I opted to forego this mode of data collection. Moreover, I did have occasion to talk informally with women I assumed were *jineteras* (given their age, foreign dates, and other observable factors); the women also thought I was a *jinetera* since I was in attendance with foreign men. Because I did not initiate my interview protocol or informed consent, I do not include those conversations in my data.

6. When the police approached our group as we left the club, her jittery reaction led me to believe she was a new or occasional *jinetera* rather than a *chica* or a prostitute.

7. "Sharking" is a British/European expression for actively pursuing sex.

8. Nadine Fernández (1999) proposes that the concept of *jineteando* needs to be expanded to incorporate "any activity outside of one's salaried employment that generates hard currency or the possibility of foreign travel … in other words, any attempt to integrate oneself into the global market economy at whatever level and through whatever means" (85).

9. I stayed in nine different hotels over the course of my research; however, I cannot count the many hotels I have visited (for interviews, drinks, dancing, etc.) during my many trips to Cuba.

10. Soon after Raul Castro assumed Cuba's leadership in early 2008, one of the much discussed reforms he introduced was opening hotels to Cuban guests who are willing to pay the full (foreign) price. As is discussed in the epilogue, many Cubans perceive the change to be insignificant because they still cannot afford to pay the convertible currency rates on their low peso salaries.

11. Dominican accents are said to be quite similar to the slower speech of Orientales (those from the eastern part of the island). I was regularly presumed to be from Santiago-de-Cuba. At one point, I spoke with a man from Pinar del Rio, in western Cuba, who spoke with what I thought was a French clip; I asked if he was Haitian.

12. Resistant to biological explanations of difference, I continue to rationalize that it must have been my vegetarianism—pork is a staple in the Cuban diet. One local explanation I have heard has to do with reproducing in an island context with few outside influences; I find this explanation unconvincing because Cuba has historically received many immigrants from and has been extremely integrated with many parts of the world.

13. While I have argued that almost all Cubans are engaged in a daily *lucha* or struggle to meet their household needs, a select group who regularly interact

with foreign tourists refer to themselves euphemistically as *luchadores*; other Cubans refer to this group as *jineteros* (hustlers).

14. She was not soliciting; on one occasion when I joined the entertainers in a night out on the town, I ended up paying Cari's way home because the Mexican men she had been dancing with all night left her otherwise stranded when she would not accompany any of them to their hotel rooms.

CHAPTER 5

Of Shorts and Segregated Socialism

For a fieldworker studying tourism in Cuba, one might expect the most enjoyable aspects of the research to have been sipping umbrella cocktails poolside or learning the intricacies of salsa in a nightclub. While I admit to engaging in such enviable activities in the name of research, my most cherished moments in the field were with retirement-aged women who showered me with information on life and love and Cuba.

Within moments of meeting Abuela Saida—the octogenarian who lived across the street from me with her 64-year-old daughter, 35-year-old granddaughter, and 13- and 6-year-old great-granddaughters—I was given an abbreviated version of her life story, which I would learn more extensively later. She introduced herself as an 80-year-old *guajira* (peasant) from Contra Maestra, telling me that she had birthed her first child while very young. She further explained that her granddaughter and great-grandchildren were well educated "to *secondaria* and *pre-universitaria*" (middle and high school), while she herself had learned to sign her name only when she was a *jovencita* of about 19 years old. In time, I would learn that this comparison between herself and her progeny shaped her zeal for Cuba's socialist revolution.

At the time, she continued chattering: "We don't have much money, but...lack of money doesn't make you poor. Here we live happy...we may not have much, but everyone has food to eat every day, and everyone has clothes to wear and a place to live. But, *bueno*, there's good and bad every-where...." As she continued to gush, she turned the topic to Cuba's then longtime leader: "It's like *El Hombre*, Fidel—how I love that man!! While other leaders shame their people, ours never has. He's always honorable and makes us proud." Before Abuela Saida bid me farewell that first after-noon, she told me that she hoped Americans would be able to come to

Cuba again; and then, with momentary nostalgia for the prerevolutionary period, she added, "I remember before, when there used to be plenty
of Americans here, walking around in their shorts. There was so much
money then...."

In her introduction, Abuela Saida invoked a discourse that I heard
from numerous individuals who were at least in their teens when the revolution triumphed in 1959. They were old enough to recognize the changes
that occurred in their native country, and most of them were reportedly
more than satisfied with those changes. Another example is Tía Caridad's
musings (see chapter 2) about how her involvement in the revolution's
Literacy Campaign changed her life. Mona Rosendahl (1997) discusses
memories of *antes*—before the revolution—as being a significant factor
in the longevity of Cuba's revolutionary project. Because many of Cuba's
poorest people saw an increased standard of living under the revolution,
they have continued to support it through high and low points.

Certainly there are many for whom Fidel Castro and his socialist
experiment did not bring benefits but signified loss of property, status, and
rights. I interviewed only two such individuals in Cuba, each coinciden-
tally a medical professional—a doctor and a dentist. Both men described
the roles they had played in the revolutionary war and said they believed
the changes would benefit greater numbers than they harmed. They also
believed that their skills could be of service to the new system. As the dentist told his story, I noted that his wife sat with her hands on her lap looking away from him. I would later learn that the couple had a son living in
Miami and that she had pleaded with her husband to leave the country on
several occasions. Indeed, most Cubans who saw significant downward
mobility have long since gone into exile and do not have a voice in the
country today.

However, the exiles' silence does not mean they do not have a significant presence in Cuba. Beyond their influence on U.S. policy toward Cuba,
the fact that so many people on the island have family members who live
allá (over there, generally indicating Miami) means that their virtual presence is always highly palpable. Especially in the post-Soviet era, when hardship became the norm, many members of the younger generations—very
young or unborn when the revolution triumphed—have begun to recon-
sider the benefits of Cuban socialism (Domínguez García 1997; see also
Dolgin and Franco 1993). In a rare weak moment after a particularly difficult day, Yeshua once said, "I know the revolution has changed my mother's
world, but what has it done to mine?" In chapter 2, Tía Caridad talked about
how Yeshua and Hermina would be "nothing" without the revolution, but
here we see her nephew rhetorically asking, "What has the revolution done

for me lately?" For youth who have lived their entire lives with the benefits of the revolution's social system, the Special Period provided a reality check of sorts. Rather than blindly clinging to their (grand)parents' memories of *antes*, a new generation of Cubans now must determine whether the system they have always known is worth maintaining or not.

Abuela Saida recalled the wealth proffered by tourists of a bygone era who walked around in shorts when the Cubans who served them could not; Mami Teresa once proudly asserted that it was the revolutionary government that legislated Cubans' right to wear shorts as well. Much like the colored resort bracelets described in chapter 4, shorts represented leisure—service workers (and their fellow citizens) had to dress respectfully in skirts or long pants. But today's youth want more than shorts, and many are trading in the postsecondary education of which their parents are so proud for the more lucrative lifestyles offered through hustling (Díaz-Briquets 1993; Domínguez García 1997). If, in the past, tourists brought wealth while Cubans humbly served them, today's *jineteros* are not so humble in their quest for a share of the global capital in their midst.

Separate and Unequal

One argument underlying this book is that the Cuban government believes the secret to maintaining socialist values amid encroaching capitalism is to keep the two conceptual worlds as separate as possible: the peso economy is for Cubans and the hard currency economy is for foreigners. Tourists should ideally stay in hotels in which the only Cubans with whom they come in contact are "good revolutionaries" who are willing to be invisible to their foreign visitors. Tourists should see only the side of "Cuba" that the Cuban government desires them to see.

One problem with this approach is that many of the tourists who come to Cuba are seeking a degree of Cuban "authenticity" (see MacCannell 1976). While the absence of Americans and U.S. global entities like McDonald's certainly play a part, some define this illusory authenticity in terms of bucolic agricultural imagery, others in terms of political fantasies about the revolution (or its insignificance), and many have racial or cultural fantasies about the "nature" of the Cuban people. In their quest for authenticity, they want to stay in a "real Cuban" home, eat "real Cuban" food, and make "real Cuban" friends. Those Cubans who seek to accommodate such tourist desires encounter such barriers as taxes on formal participation in the tourist industry (through *casas particulares* and *paladar* home restaurants) or harassment, fines, or even arrest for informal participation (*jineterismo*). The tourists themselves rarely are penalized.

Another problem with the attempt at separating the Cuban world from the tourist world is that some Cubans have access to hard currency. The government is well aware of this; in fact, one of the primary reasons the government opted to legalize the possession of dollars for Cubans in August 1993 was that—because of **remittances** from Cubans living abroad and shortages of necessary goods in central warehouses—more hard currency was circulating in the underground economy than in the official economy. The government's solution was to legalize the possession of dollars, while continuing to discourage citizens from pursuing luxuries on the revolution's moralistic grounds. Spanish tourist Grace captured the essence of the socialist dilemma: "It is very good in theory to have all of your basic needs met, but shouldn't there be quality of life too?" Article 43 of the Cuban Constitution clearly states that all citizens may "be served at all restaurants and other public service establishments" and "enjoy the same resorts, beaches, [and] parks" (Cuban Constitution 1992; see Figure 5.1). This law—initially aimed against racial discrimination—is now interpreted to allow distinguishing between "citizens" and foreigners. In effect, the Cuban government has substituted one form of racial discrimination for another by superimposing the tourist enclave industry on top of revolutionary socialist ideals.

Most significantly, therefore, the operational problem with this segregationist policy is how to determine fairly who belongs in which category.

FIGURE **5.1   Building hotels for socialism (photo by the author)**

The billboard in the foreground reads, "I Love/Want You Free"; the distant billboard to the right (with the image of Ché Guevara at the end) reads, "Juntos seguiremos luchando por un mundo mejor / Together we will continue fighting for a better world."

Foreigners and Cubans are identified primarily from visual cues like skin color, hair and clothing styles, and overall comportment. Only when those initial identifiers prove ambiguous are such secondary identifiers as idiom and accent scrutinized. Whereas the Cubans one encounters on the street may engage in this kind of inquiry out of genuine curiosity or with the hope of some form of financial gain, gatekeepers in official capacities similarly read embodied nationalities in order to determine who belongs in the tourist world and who does not. Cubans are thereby excluded from the spaces of luxury reserved for foreign tourists, in a fundamentally unequal treatment that amounts to the same kind of discrimination that the revolution claims to seek to eliminate.

Rather than evolving into the raceless, classless (male) protector of the (female) Cuban nation it had long claimed itself to be, since the post-Soviet Special Period the revolutionary government has effectively "darkened" and "feminized" the Cuban populace through its quest for global capital in the tourism industry. Though they are generally reluctant to admit it because of the earlier advances made under the revolution, blacks and women now recognize that the security promised by the socialist revolution has weakened as supporters and detractors alike have been forced to *luchar*—to survive by any means—on a daily basis (see Bengelsdorf 1997). The leadership's moralistic stance has begun to ring hollow among a people who have been forced to lie, steal, and hustle in order to achieve a decent standard of living. While many people still believe in the ideals of the revolution, most have begun to question the possibility of fully realizing it given that the best the country has to offer is now reserved for foreign tourists.

Transition or Transformation?

The Cuban government long expressed paranoia about the possibility that another U.S. invasion would attempt to overthrow the socialist revolution like the 1961 Bay of Pigs. Under the presidency of George W. Bush (elected largely by the anti-Castro Cuban vote in Florida), and during the "war on terrorism" enacted in Afghanistan and Iraq following the attacks of September 11, 2001, that paranoia found a degree of substance. Soon after Bush took office, he replaced the head of the U.S. **Interest Section** in Cuba (the de facto diplomatic office that substitutes for an embassy) with James Casan, an aggressive anticommunist who immediately began irritating his Cuban hosts by holding parties and inviting dissidents as though they were representatives of the Cuban state. Eventually, the dissidents were permitted to meet in Casan's home, where they would be protected from

Cuban vigilance by diplomatic immunity. In reprisal, the Cuban government began restricting the movements of members of the U.S. diplomatic
corps in Havana, and later expelling them. The U.S. government matched
these moves with restrictions on members of the Cuban Interest Section in
Washington, DC, as well as Cuban diplomats posted to the United Nations
in New York. Relations between the two countries nearly broke down
entirely during this period (Pérez and Schoultz 2003). At the time of this
writing, Cuban–U.S. relations remain contentious, even amid rising hopes
for changes in U.S.–Cuban relations with the election of Barack Obama to
the presidency in November 2008.

All of this pressure from the United States—like the almost fifty-year
blockade between the two countries—has been called an attempt to force
a "transition" from socialism to democratic capitalism.[1] The literature on
postsocialism usefully illuminates how discourses that describe *transi-
tions* to capitalism might benefit by instead considering *transformations* in
socialism. Whereas "transition" implies an evolutionary teleology—with
the value placed on the "end stage" in relation to the "previous stage"—
"transformation" views change as part of a process whose eventual forms
are not yet known (Burawoy and Verdery 1999).

For nearly two decades now, many around the world have admired
Cuba's revolution for its attempt to ideologically stand up to the capitalist
empire. As historian Marifeli Pérez-Stable writes,

> In August 1990, when the government declared the special period in
> peacetime, it signaled a commitment to socialism against all odds.
> The special period was an attempt to reinsert the Cuban economy
> into the world economy without relinquishing socialism and relin-
> quishing national sovereignty to the United States. If successful,
> such a transition would, indeed, be as extraordinary as that which
> Cuba had achieved during the early 1960s.
>
> *(Pérez-Stable 1993, 158)*

The revenue generated by the tourism industry during the Special
Period has supported the Cuban government's aspiration of participating
in the capitalist global economy while maintaining a socialist domestic
doctrine. A key question that *Cuban Color* raises is whether socialist ideology is compatible with capitalist practices not only at the systemic level but
also at the level of everyday citizens. The peso-dollar dual economy values
convertible currency over domestic pesos; the socialist–capitalist dual ideology caters to white(ned) foreign tourists and excludes black(ened) Cuban
residents. While the hard currency generated by the former is meant to
sustain the social system featuring free education and health care for the

benefit of the latter, as with so many other aspects of the Special Period, the Cuban people are often forced to swallow their collective pride in the name of the revolution.

Conclusion

This research project began with the question, "Does tourism in today's Special Period threaten Cuba's socialist revolution?" I found that though people may not consciously think in racial terms on a day-to-day basis, social status continues to be understood racially as it was before the revolution. Moreover, these Cuban understandings of race and place were replicated—and institutionalized and magnified—when foreign tourists were added to the picture. Like *negros*, all Cubans were understood to be of secondary importance and of a lower status than were their (comparably) white foreign tourist counterparts.

The creation of a peso-dollar dual economy opened up crevices between two distinct modes of existence in Cuba—one of difficulty and *lucha*, the other of comfort and comparative luxury. Remittances from exiles remain the largest source of hard currency for ordinary people, but tourism represents a more measurable, less ideologically suspect mode that attracts *divisa* directly to the state and, sometimes illicitly, to the Cuban people. By segregating citizens from foreign tourists, tourism magnifies the differences between the haves and the have-nots even more than do remittances. Moreover, the transnational dynamic implies that even the wealthiest Cubans are more *atrasado* (literally, "backwards" or further behind) than their foreign guests, an observation that in the Cuban context racializes Cubans as *negro* (black) and tourists as *blanco* (white).

While the revolutionary government has called the social division that accompanies dollarization and tourism a "necessary evil" (Jatar-Hausmann 1999), the commodification of Cuban culture and identity that coincides with tourism may challenge the revolution's central objective of self-determination. As Jacqui Alexander (1997) argues, "the imperial practice" of tourism erodes national identity because it involves "the production of a specific cultural form dutifully chiseled from a mold produced *elsewhere*" (Alexander 1997, 96). Hosts to tourism—in Cuba as well as in other sites of international tourism—meet the raced and gendered expectations of Western tourists through their work in the service sector and the entertainment sphere, as well as through sexual representations in tourism (Kempadoo 1999). While Afro-Cuban culture is now recognized as a key part of Cuban national culture (in part because of the prerevolutionary tourism industry), cultural tourism today acts like a museum in many ways, reviving the most marketable aspects of Cuba's past—especially with regard to the roles of blacks and women—and placing them on display for a foreign audience (see Comaroff and Comaroff 2009). Indeed, this kind of "consumption of culture" that is endemic to tourism is a common characteristic throughout the Caribbean (Sheller 2003).

Yet, even as governments throughout the region have been encouraged by global financial institutions (the International Monetary Fund, the World Bank, the Inter-American Development Bank) to participate in touristic enterprises that exploit local labor, cultural, and natural resources in order to secure the loans needed to stay (barely) afloat in the global economy (Dupuy 2001), the most greatly underserved members of Caribbean societies often creatively manipulate this culture commodification for personal gain (Kempadoo 1999). All manner of hustlers and higglers seek their share of the global capital that arrives on the shores of the Caribbean with foreigners. In the Cuban case, as the government strives to limit capitalism to the official tourism sector while it still does not receive assistance from international lending organizations, *jineteros* and *bisneros* represent an emerging spirit of entrepreneurship that challenges the revolution's socialist ideals. Indeed, the more Cuba reintegrates itself into the capitalist global economy through tourism, the more closely its cultural, economic, and political future parallels that of the rest of the Caribbean—a future in which the needs and aspirations of the nation's citizens are contrasted with the dictates of the many incarnations (the IMF/World Bank, the United States, affluent tourists) of foreign capital.

*   *   *

During a taxi ride from my hotel to the airport, I had a noteworthy conversation with the *chofer* (driver). He wanted to know if what the Cuban press said about the United States was true. He asked if there was racism in the United States. I told him there was. After we had gotten into more specifics—about the prospects for interracial marriage, jobs, housing, and the prominence of such personalities as Colin Powell and Michael Jordan—he eventually clarified why he was asking. The *chofer*, a black man, had been a professor of engineering at the University of Havana. He told me that he believed life was better in the United States and that he would get there someday. Comparatively, according to him, Cuba's only redeeming quality is its minimal violence. Having arrived at the airport, he let me out of the cab and refused my tip; he then concluded our conversation by telling me that he hoped to see me in the United States someday.

I have written this book not only for the many Americans who have difficulty recognizing the subtleties of life in Cuba because of blockaded information, but also for this gentleman—as well as many other Cubans I met on the island and in exile. I hope that *Cuban Color* has clarified that Cuba is a colorful place, featuring brilliant and creative people; yet, at the same time, Cuba's color also comes in darker shades characterized by touristic racialization and by the day-to-day *lucha* to survive.

Note

1. Perhaps because allusions to "freedom" are more justifiable, the political question of democracy is always emphasized more than the economic question of capitalism that I perceive to be truly at issue. As Alex Dupuy puts it, "whether a government is democratic or not is ultimately immaterial to the international financial institutions. What really matters to them is that the state, particularly in the peripheral or semiperipheral countries, behaves or can be made to behave as a 'market friendly' state" (Dupuy 2001, 532).

Where Are They Now?

I had not traveled to Cuba exclusively for research in six years when I visited Central Havana in the summer of 2007. This time, I had no family business, since my marriage had dissolved a few years earlier. My objective was to learn how life in Cuba may have changed in light of Fidel Castro's illness and his brother Raul's impending succession to the leadership.

Unable to contact my preferred *casa particular* by telephone from the United States, I reserved a room at the Hotel Popular, located some fifty feet from María and Pepe's home, with a plan to relocate once I had talked to my old friends in person. The couple had been one of the most efficient teams I had ever observed in the course of my fieldwork. They both seemed to be equally invested in their bed-and-breakfast business, with her cooking wonderful meals while he ensured that the house was always presentable for guests. In most *casas* where I lived, housework was feminized, but Pepe was as likely to cut vegetables in preparation for the meals as he was to mop the floors or sweep the outside walk.

After dropping my suitcase off in my hotel room, I headed immediately to their house, even before eating. When I could not locate the unobtrusive doorbell tourists rang to seek a room, I was forced to ask the teenaged girl in the window next door how to contact María and Pepe. She indicated that I should check across the street on the Malecón wall. Confused, I turned around to see Mario, the couple's housekeeper, who immediately recognized me and began to dodge oncoming traffic until we were face to face.

We greeted with *besito* air-kisses as he caught me up on four years of occurrences in forty seconds. Apparently, Pepe had gone to Miami in October 2003 to visit family and had never returned. In March 2004 María—though still married to Pepe and pregnant with his child—had married a Swiss man and immigrated to Switzerland with their older daughter, Vidailis, now 22. Though Pepe was reportedly miserable in the United States and wanted to return to his house in Havana, María was trying to get a U.S. visa for Vidailis, the baby she had since delivered, and herself so that the family could be reunited. Mario was careful to communicate that the entire maneuver was a ploy the family had come up with to get out of Cuba; the only thing that remained unclear was whether or not the Swiss husband was knowingly party to a marriage of convenience.

Thus began my week of seeking former contacts, and thus it continued. My next quest was for one of my earliest collaborators—Javier, the Rastafarian. I sat in our meeting spot on the Malecón, where he once told me I could always find him. Instead, I was overlooked for hours by the many Rastas and apparent *jineteros* who walked by, until a character who called himself "Pipo de Caja Quinta" approached with that familiar old question, "*¿Qué hora es?*" that hustlers use to feel out a foreigner. We struck up a conversation in which I told him of my purpose. He went right to work locating some old-time hustlers to figure out Javier's whereabouts. We finally got the word from an older hustler named Antonio that my friend sounded familiar, but all of the genuine Rastas "*se fueron*" (had left). Now there were just the young kids who wore their hair in dreadlocks to attract foreign women.

So Pipo, a 35-year-old ex-convict from rural Havana, became my new source of information. He and his best friend, El Duque, listened to my theories—about *la lucha* and the racialized practices surrounding tourism—and corrected me where they thought I was off. But they gave me the most important endorsement I could ask for when I explained my racial theory of Cuban tourism and they told me, "You really understand what's going on here!" Pipo introduced me to all the hustlers worth knowing, and we held a focus group about their motives for hustling on the Malecón on the eve of my departure. They also updated me on all the latest street terminology, some of which I think is particularly relevant to the changes in Cuba today.

From *Jineteros* to *Perros Callejeros*

Throughout this book, I have argued that *jineteros* are rather nonthreatening hustlers who are merely trying to acquire global capital for individual and family sustenance. I suggested in chapter 5 that this group might constitute a future business class, given their customer orientation and entrepreneurial spirit. This may have been true of *jineteros*, but as my quest for Javier suggests, they are a rapidly disappearing breed that is being replaced by young men known popularly as *perros callejeros* (street dogs), whose desperate pursuit of *fula* (hard currency) has replaced the more gamesman-like interchange of *jineteros* of five years earlier. These new "street dogs" congregate in "packs" but hold little allegiance to pack (or any) relationships—indeed, they reportedly turn on one another with little provocation.

As the evening hours grow later, the Malecón fills with increasing numbers of these dreadlocked faux-Rasta youths, who range in age from approximately 15 to 25 (about the same age as the *jineteros* I had known earlier). In the past, Rastas congregated particularly on an east-facing bench in Havana's Parque Central; though many of them also played up their Rasta image in order to benefit from tourists, their fellow Cubans still associated them with the broader Rastafarian black nationalist ideology. So I was shocked when, in response to Pipo's frequent game of having those to whom I was introduced guess where I was from, one young dread spat at my feet as he said: "Who cares? Some sh_tty country," and continued with an ugly tirade about "poor countries full of stinky black people." When Pipo finally informed him that I was from the United States, he smiled broadly, introduced himself in English, and extended his hand for me to shake. He could not understand why I refused until I admonished him in Spanish, explaining that I had understood every antiblack, un-Rasta-like thing he had said. In the past, my dreadlocks would have been enough to earn an embrace of fellowship from any Rasta to whom I was introduced. This time, my black skin and hairstyle were interpreted as signaling the poverty of a developing country unworthy of his attention, whether African or Caribbean—at least until the truth of my origins was revealed.

Also, whereas the *jineteros* of the past remained well integrated within their households, many of the so-called *perros callejeros* have been thrown out of their homes because of their antisocial behavior. One night, Pipo asked a young man who had been huddled under his own shirt, shivering in his sleep a few feet from our seat on the Malecón, what was wrong; the youth told us he was sick. Pipo later whispered to me that just minutes earlier, the teenager's mother had walked past him as if he were a stranger.

In my previous research, no one I interviewed ever called themselves a *jinetero/a*; they always used the euphemism "*luchador(a)*." During my focus group on the street, the young men identified themselves clearly as "a *jinetero*" or "a so-called *perro callejero*," indicating to me a shift from more subtle forms of *lucha* to more pointed lifestyles based in illegal practices.

Yumas Out, *Pepes* In

If *yuma* was the colloquial term for foreigners with money five years ago, the new terms—*pieza* and *pepe*—signify a specific focus on the money foreigners represent. *Pieza* translates literally as "piece," and in one sense is used much as youths in the U.S. might talk about a sexually available individual (usually female) as a "piece of _ss." It seems that hustlers interpret tourists to be bringing their money to Cuba for the taking. Or as Duque put it, "they know they've got it and they know we want it, we just have to figure out how to get it from them." Indeed, a new verb has been created to describe this quest to manipulate tourists into spending their money to the hustler's benefit: *mecaniquiarse* involves the hustler making a series of suggestions to tourists that ultimately lead to a commission. Another usage of *pieza* means "mark," as in someone a con man marks for a planned heist.

The other new term for foreigner is *pepe* (and its feminine *pepa*), which translates as a prostitute's customer (a john). Like the shift from *jinetero* to *perros callejeros*, calling tourists *pepes* and *pepas* removes the soft edges allowed by *yuma*. The new term highlights the commercial nature of the tourist–Cuban interaction, but it does involve an important departure from perceptions of prostitution as a practice that objectifies "the prostitute" (i.e., the Cuban); here, the *pepe* or *pepa* is the objectified *pieza*. In this way Cubans maintain some of the sense of empowerment described in my earlier discussion of *jineteras*. Again, the most significant occurrence in the intervening years was the change in Cuba's leadership.

Raul Castro and Change

In late February 2008, Fidel Castro officially stepped down from his nearly fifty-year tenure as Cuba's president. His younger brother, Raul, was subsequently elected president by the Cuban National Assembly. This shift in leadership has precipitated a great deal of discussion in the United States about the ideological change that may be occurring in Cuba, given the relaxations Raul has allowed on Cubans' access to such luxuries as compact disc and DVD players, mobile phones, and even hotel rooms. Given the potential significance of such changes, I traveled to Cuba again in July 2008 to find out what such openings meant for everyday Cubans.

On the flight from Miami, I talked to a British diplomat who was based in Havana, thinking he would have some kind of official perspective on Raul's changes: "You know what I've noticed? Before when I would go to the gym at Hotel Lujo, men would have prostitutes in the bathroom." He paused thoughtfully before deciding, "Now, I guess it is less difficult to use the toilet." Upon landing, I saw the *chofer* who drove me from the airport to my hotel send a text message from his cell phone while we were stopped at a red light. I took the opportunity to ask about the openings Raul had introduced to Cuban society. He shrugged his shoulders as he gunned the engine: "The change is cosmetic.... Only people who had money before can afford that stuff." Likewise, one of the hustlers Pipo introduced me to later that night asserted, "They still don't want Cubans in hotels or socializing with tourists—and the workers and security treat you like you're committing a crime by being in the hotel."

It was becoming increasingly clear that Raul's leadership had fostered very little change on the ground. Indeed, Pipo usefully shared his own analysis, suggesting that permitting access to cellular phones, hotels, and other luxuries just legalized what people had been doing illegally, while making it easier for the government to harass people for their capitalistic endeavors. For example, as before, he can enter a hotel lobby to have a drink in the hotel bar with a guest. He is still discouraged from doing so alone, both by the security guard and by the hard-currency price. The difference is that if a (foreign) hotel guest wants to invite a Cuban to their room they can pay the double occupancy room rate for the Cuban guest so he or she can spend the night. The state benefits from the additional money, but afterward the police know exactly where to find the individual who broke the *andando con turista* edict, from the ID number they must provide upon check-in. He argued that cellular phones are similar, reiterating what the taxi driver and other hustlers had said about the financial impediments: "The phone service costs $120 CUC, the activation card costs $20 CUC, and the pay-as-you-go card costs another $20. Only very few Cubans can afford that."

Perhaps the last person I talked to said it best: "Sure there've been changes, but to tell you the truth, if I had enough money to stay in that hotel, I'd rather use it to leave this place!" In other words, it is so expensive to take advantage of the relaxations on hotels, DVDs, and cellular phones that it is a rare Cuban who would waste that kind of money on luxuries.

Cuban society has been changing rapidly since the fall of the Soviet Union. In the aftermath of the nationwide crisis known as the Special Period, Raul Castro has replaced his brother, Fidel, as Cuba's longtime leader, and Barack Obama promised changes in U.S. policy toward Cuba in his historic presidential campaign. Though it remains unclear how the future will play out, for the time being—with regard to tourism—Cubanness and foreignness continue to constitute separate spheres of belonging in Cuba, and those spheres continue to be interpreted in terms of Cuban racial understandings. Cubans who now enjoy luxury goods and services must also be evaluated according to whether they are wealthier white(ned) Cubans or members of the darker hustling class. Moreover, at the same time that Cubans have been permitted greater access to material goods and services, some of those who cannot get legitimate access are shifting to strategies that involve a more hardened form of *lucha*. Though Cuba's future complexion remains to be determined, for the time being—and for the majority of Cubans—*sigue la lucha*—the struggle continues.

Colonial Era

1400s

| Oct 1492 | Christopher Columbus arrives in eastern Cuba and claims the land for Spain |

1500s

| 1510s | Discovery of gold turns Spanish attention away from Caribbean to North and South American mainlands |

1600s

| | Cuban development of a mixed-race peasant society |

1700s

| June 1762 | British capture Havana (but exchange it for Florida in 1763) and initiate mass importation of African slaves to Cuba; exclusive trade relations between Cuba and Spain end |
| 1791–1795 | Slave insurrection in neighboring Saint Domingue begins the Haitian revolution; thousands of French slaveholders flee to Cuba with their slaves |

1800s

| Oct 1868 | Carlos Manuel de Céspedes frees his slaves and enlists them into the rebel army initiating Cuba's independence movement |
| 1886 | Slavery officially abolished in Cuba |

| Jan 1898 | USS Maine explodes in Havana Harbor; United States blames Spain, beginning Spanish-American War |
| Dec 1898 | Treaty of Paris transfers authority over Cuba, Puerto Rico, Guam, and the Philippines to the United States |

Republican Era

1900s

Feb 1901	Cuban Constitution, modeled after U.S. constitution, incorporates provisions of Platt Amendment allowing U.S. intervention in Cuban affairs and leasing Guantanamo Bay naval base to United States
1933	Provisional "government of 100 days" abrogates the Platt Amendment and makes reforms including women's right to vote; United States opposes reforms and supports another military coup
1940	Batista elected 14th president of Cuba; Constitution of 1940 adopted
1952	Three months before Cuba's June elections, Batista overturns the 1940 constitution by staging a coup
July 26, 1953	Fidel Castro and supporters unsuccessfully attack the Moncada military barracks in Santiago-de-Cuba
1956	The Moncada survivors, now known as the Movimento de 26 Julio (July 26th Movement), return to Cuba; some escape Batista's men into the Sierra Maestra, where they are joined by an impromptu rebel militia

Revolutionary Era

Jan 1, 1959	Batista flees the country; U.S. government recognizes the new Cuban government within a week
Feb 1959	Fidel Castro becomes prime minister of Cuba
Summer 1960	Revolutionary government nationalizes U.S. oil refineries
Fall 1960	Cuba nationalizes all U.S. banks, several sugar mills, other large U.S.-owned industries
Jan 1961	U.S. severs diplomatic relations with Cuba; Cuban literacy campaign begins
March 1962	U.S. embargo on Cuba is expanded; rationing begins in Cuba

1970	Failure to meet 10-million-ton target for sugar harvest effectively links Cuban economy to Soviet Union
1991	Soviet troops leave Cuba; when the Soviet Union disbands at the end of the year, Cuba loses its annual $6 billion subsidy; Castro declares "Special Period in a Time of Peace"
1993	Cuba legalizes use of U.S. currency, which remains in circulation until October 2004
May 2004	U.S. announces tougher sanctions limiting family travel to every 3 years and limiting family remittances
Oct 2004	Cuba ends circulation of the U.S. dollar, replacing it with the *peso convertible*
Feb 2008	Fidel Castro announces he will not accept the upcoming nomination for the presidency; the National Assembly unanimously elects Raul Castro

For a detailed timeline see http://www.historyofcuba.com/history/time/timetbl1.html.

Chapter 1

Exercises

1. *Race beyond Color*: Write a narrative that describes your earliest as well as your most recent recognition of race. In each case, what made the incident racial? Have you encountered similar circumstances that you did not consider racial? Were the racial dynamics different, or did the reaction/behavior change?

2. *Reflexive journal*: In a notebook or on your computer, begin to journal your knowledge of Cuba. Begin before you have read any further: Before taking this course or reading this book, what was your image of Cuba? What is the source of that image? Continue to write in your journal about your changing conceptions of Cuba as you read.

Additional Resources

Latin American Network Information Center (LANIC). *Castro Speech Database* (http://lanic.utexas.edu/la/cb/cuba/castro.html). Searchable database of the full, translated text of speeches by Fidel Castro from 1959 to 1996. Also provides links to other sources for Castro speeches.

Black, S. *Life and Debt* (New York: Tuff Gong Pictures, 2001). Using a Jamaican example, this film graphically illustrates how the free trade policies of international lending organizations affect the economies and people of developing countries.

Chapter 2

Exercises

1. *Race Debate on the United States*: Chapter 2 has provided descriptions of some well-known Cuban tropes involving race and/or gender (i.e., *Guajiros, La Mulata, Guapos*), this in a society that is generally conceived as nonracist. How is gendered race discussed in the United States, a country with a long history of racial animosity? Consider the local news, popular blogs, and social networking interactions. Recalling the PIC of 1912, does a silence (or lack of active discussion) about race mean it is not relevant? Take note of your observations and be prepared to engage a class discussion mediated by your instructor.

2. *Journal Reflection*: Go to any grocery or drug store and look for images of nonwhite people on products. Where and how is blackness portrayed? Racial mixture? Asian-ness? Hispanic-ness? Do female or male images predominate? Hypothesize about how nonwhites are marketed. Write the results in your journal and begin to pay attention to nonwhite representations on television and in print media.

Additional Resources

AfroCubaWeb (http://www.afrocubaweb.com/). Web site promotes Afro-Cuban culture, including music and the arts, publications, lectures, conferences, and videos. Focus on disseminating information from Cuba to global audience.

Rolando, G. *Raices de mi Corazón* [*Roots of my Heart*] (Imagines del Caribe: Havana, 2001). A film that depicts a black Cuban woman's personal quest to understand the silence surrounding her unknown grandfather until it is revealed that he was killed with thousands of black men seeking political representation in the "Little War of 1912."

Chapter 3

Exercises

1. *Special Period*: How much money do you spend in a week? What do you spend it on? What aspects of your life require money to keep things going smoothly? Beginning tomorrow morning, for the next seven days begin trying to answer these questions. Keep track of all of your expenditures, noting whether you used cash, check, or some form of plastic (debit/credit). Note the country or city of origin for the goods you buy. Consider your mode(s) of transportation, including those that may be subsidized, like a bus pass provided by your school or job. After the week tracking your expenditures, take half of what you spent the previous week from the bank and use only that money for all of your expenditures, use a less expensive

mode of transportation, and stop buying products from the country or city you use most frequently. Disconnect your electronics (television, lamps, remove light bulbs) in the morning before you begin your day. Leave them off for an hour or two when you return home. After you have all gone through your brief "Special Period," discuss the experience as a class: What aspects of the Cuban Special Period did this exercise replicate? What cannot be replicated?

2. *Cuban Links to the World*: As an individual or in pairs, access at least two Web sites from the Additional Resources listed hereafter. How do they differ from one another? Who is the audience for each? How does the site's content contribute to your understanding of daily life in Cuba based on the material in chapter 3? Write about your findings or discuss them with your partner.

Additional Resources

Beautiful Me(s) (http://www.beautifulmes.com/story.html). Documentary about American Ivy League students who travel to Cuba and have a transformative experience, feeling more welcomed there than they do in their home country. Web site and various links promote screenings of the film.

Generation Y Blogsite (http://desdecuba.com/generationy/). A dissident blog from inside Cuba about the difficulties of day-to-day life.

Granma International (http://www.granma.cu/ingles/). The international edition of the official newspaper of the Cuban government. Though the international edition is not identical to the local, hard-copy edition, the online source provides insight into locally filtered news reporting.

Cuban Radio and Television (http://www.digiradio.ch/radiocuba/). Live digital streams of Cuban television and radio provide insight into entertainment and news options. Programming may be off the air during late-night hours, especially for television.

Chapter 4

Exercises

1. *Color and Privilege*: As an individual or in pairs, conduct a Web search on tropical tourism (see "Additional Resources" regarding Cuba). What images predominate for the Caribbean? How do they differ (if at all) from imagery of the Pacific islands? When there are people in photographic images, how would you describe their skin colors or "race"? Do you believe the images represent tourists or the toured? Why? Begin to notice skin color imagery in tourism advertising for tourism to other regions.

2. *Tourist for a Day*: Consult your local visitor's bureau to find ways to be a tourist where you live. As an individual, in pairs, or as a class, take a bus

tour, go to a museum or restaurant, or stroll through a mall. Pay attention to interactions between workers and visitors to consider the balance of power: does it lie with the consumers and their spending power, the workers and their directive power, or somewhere in between? Return to discuss findings as a group. Individuals with experience in the worker roles should share their knowledge from both perspectives.

Additional Resources

Cuba.com (http://www.cuba.com/). Web site about Cuba with heavy tourism advertisements. Purports to be unaffiliated with any nation.

CubaWeb (http://www.cubaweb.cu/eng). Web site marketing tourism in Cuba provides perspective on what Cuban government believes tourists seek in tour experience.

Chapter 5

Exercises

1. *Three Generations on Cuba*: Choose three individuals of different generations to interview: (1) college age, (2) parents' age, (3) grandparents' age. Ask each about their perceptions of Cuba. What is the source of those perceptions (news, personal experience, hearsay, etc.)? Write an analysis that considers the similarities and/or differences among the generations. Alternately, your instructor may choose to have the class discuss your findings as a group.

2. *Journal Reflection*: Revisit your first journal assignment. How has your perspective on Cuba been challenged, reinforced, or changed by the material presented in this book? What is your image of Cuba now?

Additional Resource

Dolgin, G., and V. Franco, *Cuba Va* (San Francisco, CA: Cuba Va Film Project, 1993). Documentary portrays unfiltered Cuban youth perspectives on Cuban society during the Special Period. Illustrates a wide array of opinions and debates among young adults.

Commoditization (also commodification)   A commodity is an object that is bought and sold. To commoditize or commodify, then, is the process involved with turning an object into a product for purchase. Social theorist Karl Marx explains commoditization to involve assigning value to an object so that it may be exchanged; however, this "exchange value" is generally inflated beyond the object's practical usage (i.e., "use value").

Creole   In Caribbean societies, where the resident population came largely from Europe and Africa (and later Asia), each group had to adapt to the new local conditions. This process of becoming local is known as creolization. Creole, then, refers to those who have adapted to the local conditions and who identify more closely with the new locale than the old.

Cultural capital   Pierre Bourdieu's theory that describes the struggle for position between groups using culturally valuable knowledge as an exchangeable resource—that is, knowledge, experiences, and other culturally specific advantages that groups use to maintain or increase their social status. Examples familiar to most middle-class U.S. Americans include college education, travel opportunities, and club membership. Because what is considered physically attractive is culturally constructed, those preferred traits also constitute cultural capital.

Cultural construction   A collectively held belief generally perceived to be natural or inevitable that actually reflects social or cultural patterns rather than biological realities. It must be emphasized that the cultural basis of such constructions as race, gender, sexuality, religion, or eating practices does not render them at all irrelevant.

Cultural evolutionism   Cultural evolutionists believed that the differences between groups of people could change if their material conditions were changed. In other words, cultural groups were not static but could evolve depending on the extent to which they were able to meet their everyday economic needs for food, clothing, and shelter. Rather than ranking the world hierarchically by phenotype, cultural evolutionists ranked the peoples of the world according to their levels of cultural progress.

Cultural relativism   Franz Boas's school of thought conceived of cultures and peoples as equal; rather than rank groups, relativists seek to understand each culture on its own terms.

Discourse   A way of conceptualizing (especially talking or writing about) a subject. Social theorists like Michel Foucault and Judith Butler emphasize the power dynamics involved in the ways discourse establishes the parameters for how the subject can be discussed.

Essentialism   The conception that an aspect of culture (like race or gender) is fixed and unchangeable.

Ethnographic   Ethnography is the written product of anthropological (or other social science) field-based research. As an adjective, "ethnographic" indicates the ground-level focus of research that often relies on interviews and participant-observation methodology.

Global capitalism   The process called globalization has a debatably long history. The era of "global capitalism," on the other hand, is largely agreed to have begun with the fall of the Soviet Union in the late 1980s, since when capitalism has had no major competition as a political-economic system. A key feature of the global capitalist era is the increasing power of institutions representing market forces (like the International Monetary Fund and the World Bank) over nation-states. These multinational lending organizations have been criticized for pressuring relatively poor countries to adopt monetary policies (for example, devaluations of currencies) and trade policies (lowering duties on imports, not subsidizing domestic industries) that boost the profits of multinational firms.

Globalization   Globalization describes the integrated nature of the world, especially with regard to trade, finance, culture, ideas, and people. Technological innovations in communication and transportation have long played a role in linking geographically distant places.

Interest Section (U.S. or Cuban)   Because Cuba and the United States have no official diplomatic relations, Interest Sections were established during a period of dialogue under President Jimmy Carter's administration. Each is housed in the Swiss embassy to the host country.

International lending organizations   Near the end of World War II, the Allied nations created international lending organizations like the

World Bank and the International Monetary Fund to help (in particular) European countries devastated by the wars to rebuild their economies. With the independence movements of the 1960s that ended colonialism in Africa, Asia, and the Caribbean, these lending organizations financially backed emerging nations, but on terms largely more concerned with the market than with the implications for the society in question. These international lending organizations have become even more powerful since the fall of the Soviet Union, since Soviet loans are no longer available to developing countries.

Jim Crow   Within ten years of the abolition of slavery in the United States, many state and local lawmakers legalized the separation of black and white Americans in schools, restaurants, transportation, and other public spaces. These segregating policies were called "Jim Crow laws," in reference to a well-known blackface caricature from the early nineteenth century.

Leakages   In the context of tourism, leakages describe loss of potential income by host countries to such overseas entities as airlines and hotel chains.

Letter of invitation   Recognizing its citizens' lack of financial capital in an increasingly capitalist world, the Cuban government claims to seek to protect them from becoming wards of the state (i.e., welfare, incarceration) when they travel abroad by insisting that they have a letter of invitation from an individual or group in the target country. The letter promises that the party who issued the invitation will pay all expenses for the invited Cuban while in the country.

Liberalization   See **neoliberal capitalism**.

La lucha   A noun (or verb: *luchar*) that means struggle or fight. The Cuban government regularly invokes the term to signify the collective nature of the revolutionary process. Everyday Cubans use the term to describe their individualized day-to-day struggles to survive.

Machismo   Sociological label for the culturally constructed "masculine" behaviors of lower-class Latin American men. Macho or *machista* behaviors include reverence for virility, strength, honor, taking care of one's family (especially women in the family). Machismo is frequently critiqued for its phallocentric aspects like sexual indiscriminance, competition or fighting, and the desire to be in control, especially of women. While the term "machismo" was coined to label masculinism among Latin American men, there are parallel behaviors among other male groups, especially the socially disempowered.

Metropole   From the Greek, "metropole" literally translates as mother-city. In the Marxist-based World Systems approach to political economy, the metropole (or core) is conceived as the developed, industrial world, while the periphery is the underdeveloped part of the world that is exploited by the core for its resources. This metropole–periphery divide is also described in terms of the global North and South.

Neoliberal capitalism   The increasing shift of nation-states from domestically focused protectionism toward the competition of the global free-market economy.

Otherness   The practice of comparing those with whom we identify (also called Us or the Self) to groups whose lives and historical experiences we perceive to be different is known in social science research as Othering. Tourism builds on the tendency to view one's own culture as normal and those of Others as curiosities.

Participant-observation   A key anthropological research method that involves embedding oneself within the cultural group under analysis. By first watching and listening—that is, observing—researchers seek to understand the people and place under analysis. As researchers grow more familiar with the context, they begin to do what community members do. By participating in daily activities, researchers not only gain trust while being instructed in the correct way to do things, they also have the opportunity to better communicate the meanings of those cultural practices to others in the resulting ethnography (see "**ethnographic**").

Perestroika   From the Russian for "restructuring," perestroika refers to the reforms instituted by Soviet leader Mikhail Gorbachev in 1987 that ultimately led to the fall of the Soviet Union. While there were important political reforms like multicandidate Communist party elections, the economic changes—featuring joint-venture foreign investments and demand-driven production (after state quotas were met)—have parallels in Cuba's Special Period.

Performative   An approach to questions of identity that considers behaviors and actions based on expected social norms. For example, as cultural constructions, people are taught from an early age how to behave in accordance with societal expectations of their racial or gender identities.

Racial democracy   Many people in Latin American countries like Brazil, Colombia, Venezuela, and Cuba argue that their racially intermixed (mainly African, indigenous, and European) societies are free of racial discrimination and prejudice because of the (supposed) relative benevolence of the Spanish and Portuguese systems of slavery and colonialism. This argument was generally contrasted to the U.S. racial context that featured legal and institutionalized racial segregation. Brazilian sociologist Gilberto Freyre was among the first to articulate the "racial democracy" ideal in *Masters and Slaves* (1946); many scholars have since found the ideal to be a myth in the face of strong evidence of antiblack sentiment in those societies.

Ration book   Since 1962, the Cuban government has subsidized a significant percentage of each household's basic food needs—rice, beans, vegetables, potatoes, bread, eggs, and small quantities of meat—through a rationing system. While also receiving specific quotas from Cuban producers, the state purchases the goods from international providers at market rates and sells them to the Cuban people for nominal amounts. Ration books (called *la libreta*) provide information to the ration stores (known as *bodegas*) about how much each household is allowed for the month.

Reflexivity   A mode of social scientific inquiry that considers the ethnographer's position in the process of knowledge production. This mode of inquiry is driven by dialogue rather than monologue, questioning the cultural assumptions of the ethnographer as well as their fieldwork collaborators.

Remittances   Money sent by exiles/émigrés to family members who remained in the home country.

Social Darwinism   Herbert Spencer's adaptation of Charles Darwin's laws of natural selection to fit human societies; the theory advanced the hierarchical concept of "survival of the fittest" and implied that the dominance of European colonial powers proved the lighter races superior to the darker races.

Socialist system   Socialism is a political-economic system of centralized authority that (ideally) seeks to create a society grounded in "social" relations as opposed to capitalist relationships mediated by "material" goods and objects. In the early twentieth century, Vladimir Lenin adapted Karl Marx's theories about such Communist societies to the industrializing Russian reality to create the Marxist–Leninist socialism of the Soviet Union. As part of the Soviet bloc, Cuba has practiced Marxist-Leninism (adapted to Cuba's tropical, less economically developed context) since 1961.

Special Period   Between 1961 and 1989, Cuba was a member of the Soviet Union's Council for Mutual Economic Assistance (CMEA), which subsidized the economies of less developed members of the socialist bloc. The Soviet Union essentially traded oil for Cuban sugar at artificial rates. After the fall of the Soviet Union, the Cuban economy necessarily crashed, forcing people to suffer wartime hardships (food shortages, blackouts, and lack of transportation due to the absence of fuel) during the "Special Period in a Time of Peace."

Transnational   Institutions whose direct interests extend across multiple national boundaries.

Vanguard   A term used in socialist societies to distinguish the Communist Party leadership from the general populace. Because socialism seeks to eliminate the class system, this ruling elite is described as the people who best emulate the ideals of communism and who set an example for the masses—the proletariat—to follow in terms of selflessness, renunciation of materialism, and obedience to the moral and legal codes.

GLOSSARY OF KEY SPANISH/CUBAN TERMS

Blanqueamiento   Whitening; the quest to whiten oneself by assimilating to Western (white) behavioral and cultural norms, or to whiten one's offspring by procreating with a lighter complexioned person.

La Búsqueda   Literally, "the search"; the practice of using one's official government job to earn money beyond one's salary, that is, to *búscarsela.*

Casa particular   Literally, "private house"; effectively, "bed and breakfast" lodging.

Divisa   Hard currency (i.e., U.S. dollars or convertible Cuban peso).

Fula   Slang for hard currency or dollars.

Guajiro   Peasant.

Hombre(s) Nuevo(s)   New Man. Refers to Ernesto "Ché" Guevara's objective of creating a new society composed of New Men and Women who sacrificed for the greater good.

Interesados   Self-interested and materially motivated individuals.

Jinetero   Literally "jockey"; refers to street hustlers.

Jinetera   In its feminine form, these hustlers tend to be interpreted as sex workers.

Lucha   "Struggle"; can take noun or verb form (*luchar:* to struggle); refers to daily survival tactics.

Mambises   Fighters in Cuba's war for independence.

Mestizo   Racially mixed; in other Latin American countries it is used to describe European and indigenous mixtures, but in Cuba, it is a catchall, unspecified mixture.

Moneda Nacional   Cuba's national currency; US$1 = CU$25 (approx.); pesos.

Moreno   A racial description of someone as dark complexioned, that can be used for whites with dark features (hair, skin, eyes) as well as to gently, sometimes euphemistically, call a black person "dark" without offending that person.

Nivel de cultura   Cultural level, drawing from the Cultural Evolution perspective that cultures can be hierarchized progressively, so that there are high cultural levels (*alta cultura* or *de nivel alta*) and low cultural levels (*baja cultura* or *de nivel baja*).

Paladar   Family-run restaurant operating out of a private home.

Pardo   Brown, often used to describe *mulatos*, but also a broad term to describe respectable (middle to upper class) people of African descent.

Partido Independiente de Color   Independent Colored Party; a group of black and *mulato* veterans of Cuba's wars for independence who pressed for political representation by forming a political party. The PIC's refusal to disband resulted in the slaughter of thousands of black and *mulato* men.

Prieto   Dark. In contrast to *Moreno*, which is considered a gentle term for blackness, *prieto* can be intended and interpreted as more of an offense.

Yuma   Cuban slang for foreigner with money.

BIBLIOGRAPHY

Alexander, M. Jacqui. 1997. "Erotic Autonomy as a Politics of Decolonization: An Anatomy of Feminist and State Practice in the Bahamas Tourist Economy." In *Feminist Genealogies, Colonial Legacies, Democratic Futures*, edited by M. Jacqui Alexander and Chandra Talpade Mohanty, 63–100. New York: Routledge.

Appadurai, Arjun. 1996. *Modernity at Large: Cultural Dimensions of Globalization*. Minneapolis: University of Minnesota Press.

Baker, Lee D. 1998. *From Savage to Negro: Anthropology and the Construction of Race, 1896–1954*. Berkeley: University of California Press.

Bazuin, Turid. 1997. "The Political, Economic, Social and Cultural Position of Black Cuban Women since 1959 as a Critical Case Study of Gender and Ethnicity in Cuban Socialism." Master's thesis, University of Amsterdam.

Benedict, Ruth. 1940. *Race: Science and Politics*. New York: Modern Age Books.

Bengelsdorf, Carollee. 1997. "[Re]Considering Cuban Women in a Time of Troubles." In *Daughters of Caliban: Caribbean Women in the Twentieth Century*, edited by Consuelo López, 229–255. Bloomington: Indiana University Press.

Black, Stephanie. 2001. *Life and Debt*. Film. New York: Tuff Gong Pictures.

Brennan, Denise. 2008. *Intimacies: Love and Sex across Cultures*. New York: Columbia University Press.

Bruner, Edward M. 2005. *Culture on Tour: Ethnographies of Travel*. Chicago: University of Chicago Press.

Brunt, Paul, and Paul Courtney. 1999. "Host Perceptions of Sociocultural Impacts." *Annals of Tourism Research* 26 (July): 493–515.

Burawoy, Michael, and Katherine Verdery. 1999. *Uncertain Transition: Ethnographies of Change in the Postsocialist World*. New York: Rowman & Littlefield.

Byerly, Ingrid Bianca. 1996. "The Music Indaba: Music as Mirror, Mediator, and Prophet in the South African Transition from Apartheid to Democracy." PhD diss., Duke University.

Cabezas, Amalia Lucía. 1998. "Discourses of Prostitution: The Case of Cuba." In *Global Sex Workers: Rights, Resistance, and Redefinition*, edited by Kamala Kempadoo and Jo Doezema, 79–86. New York: Routledge.

Caribbean Tourism Organization. 2009. "Arrivals by Main Market." *Key Tourism Statistics* 1(1). Electronic document, http://www.onecaribbean. org/content/files/AUG21MainMarketTouristArrivals09.pdf (accessed September 9, 2009).

Casal, Lourdes. 1979. "The Position of Blacks in Cuban Society." In *The Position of Blacks in Brazilian and Cuban Society*, edited by Anani Dzidzienyo and Lourdes Casal, 11–14. London: Minority Rights Group.

Castillo Bueno, María de los Reyes. 2000. *Reyita: The Life of a Black Cuban Woman in the Twentieth Century*. Durham, NC: Duke University Press.

Castro, Fidel. 1975. *History Will Absolve Me*. La Habana: Editorial de Ciencias Sociales.

———. 1990 "Castro Reaffirms Socialism for Cubans." *LANIC Speech Database*. Electronic document, http://lanic.utexas.edu/project/castro/ db/1990/19900101.html (accessed September 9, 2009).

Cheong, So-Min, and Marc L. Miller. 2000. "Power and Tourism: A Foucauldian Observation." *Annals of Tourism Research* 27 (April): 371–390.

Clarke, Kamari M., and Deborah A. Thomas, eds. 2006. *Globalization and Race: Transformations in the Cultural Production of Blackness*. Durham, NC: Duke University Press.

Cohen, Colleen Ballerino. 1995. "Marketing Paradise, Making Nation." *Annals of Tourism Research* 22 (2): 404–421.

Comaroff, John L. and Jean Comaroff. 2009. *Ethnicity, Inc.* Chicago: University of Chicago Press.

Cuban Constitution. 1992. Electronic document, http://www.cubanet.org/ref/ dis/const_92_e.htm (accessed September 4, 2009).

Degler, Carl N. 1971. *Neither Black nor White: Slavery and Race Relations in Brazil and the United States*. New York: Macmillan.

de Kadt, Emmanuel. 1979. *Tourism: Passport to Development?* New York: Oxford University Press.

Díaz-Briquets, Sergio. 1993. "Collision Course: Labor Force and Educational Trends in Cuba." *Cuban Studies* 23: 91–112.

Dirlik, Arif. 1994. *After the Revolution: Waking to Global Capitalism*. Hanover, NH: Wesleyan University Press.

Dolgin, Gail, and Vicente Franco. 1993. *Cuba Va: The Challenge of the Next Generation*. Film. San Francisco, CA: Cuba Va Film Project.

Domínguez García, María Isabel. 1997. "Generations and Participation in Cuba." In *Cuba in the Special Period: Cuban Perspectives*. Special issue, *Studies in Third World Societies*, no. 60 (June): 1–12.

Dubisch, Jill. 1995. *A Different Place: Pilgrimage, Gender and Politics at a Greek Island Shrine*. Princeton, NJ: Princeton University Press.

Dupuy, Alex. 2001. "The New World Order, Globalization, and Caribbean Politics." In *New Caribbean Thought: A Reader*, edited by Brian Meeks and Folke Lindahl, 521–536. Kingston: University of West Indies Press.

Elinson, Hannah. 1999. "Cuba's *Jineteros*: Youth Culture and Revolutionary Ideology." *Cuba Briefing Paper Series* 20 (February). Washington, DC: Georgetown University Center for Latin American Studies.

Ellison, Ralph. 1992. *Invisible Man*. New York: Vintage. First Published 1947 by Random House.

Enloe, Cynthia. 1990. *Bananas, Beaches, and Bases: Making Feminist Sense of International Politics*. Los Angeles: University of California Press.

Fernández, Nadine. 1996. *Race, Romance, and Revolution: The Cultural Politics of Interracial Encounters in Cuba*. PhD diss., University of California–Berkeley.

———. 1999. "Back to the Future? Women, Race, and Tourism in Cuba." In *Sun, Sex, and Gold: Tourism and Sex Work in the Caribbean*, edited by Kamala Kempadoo, 81–89. Lanham, MD: Rowman & Littlefield.

———. 2010. *Revolutionizing Romance: Interracial Couples in Contemporary Cuba*. New Brunswick, NJ: Rutgers University Press.

Ferrer, Ada. 1999. *Insurgent Cuba: Race, Nation, and Revolution, 1868–1898*. Chapel Hill: University of North Carolina Press.

Foucault, Michel. 1978. *The History of Sexuality*. Translated by Robert Hurley. New York: Pantheon Books.

Freeman, Carla. 1997. "Reinventing Higglering across Transnational Zones: Barbadian Women Juggle the Triple Shift." In *Daughters of Caliban: Caribbean Women in the Twentieth Century*, edited by Consuelo López, 68–95. Bloomington: Indiana University Press.

Freyre, Gilberto. 1946. *Masters and Slaves: A Study in the Development of Brazilian Civilization*. Translated by Samuel Putnam. New York: Alfred A. Knopf.

Fuente, Alejandro de la. 2001. *A Nation for All: Race, Inequality, and Politics in Twentieth-Century Cuba*. Chapel Hill: University of North Carolina Press.

Fusco, Coco. 1998. "Hustling for Dollars: *Jineterismo* in Cuba." In *Global Sex Workers: Rights, Resistance, and Redefinition*, edited by Kamala Kempadoo and Jo Doezema, 151–166. New York: Routledge.

Galani-Moutafi, Vasiliki. 2000. "The Self and the Other: Traveler, Ethnographer, Tourist." *Annals of Tourism Research* 27 (January): 203–224.

Garcia, Cristina. 1992. *Dreaming in Cuban*. New York: Alfred A. Knopf.

Geertz, Clifford. 1973. *The Interpretation of Cultures: Selected Essays*. New York: Basic Books.

Gregory, Steven. 2003. "Men in Paradise: Sex Tourism and the Political Economy of Masculinity." In *Race, Nature, and the Politics of Difference*, edited by Donald Moore, Jake Kosek, and Anand Pandian, 323–355. Durham, NC: Duke University Press.

Guevara, Ernesto. 1965. *Socialism and Man*. Electronic document, http://
www.marxists.org/archive/guevara/1965/03/man socialism.htm (accessed
September 9, 2009).

Gurley, John G. 1975. *Challengers to Capitalism: Marx, Lenin, Stalin and Mao.*
2nd ed. New York: Norton.

Gutiérrez Alea, Tomás, and Juan Carlos Tabío. 1995. *Fresa y Chocolate*
[*Strawberry and Chocolate*]. Film. Burbank, CA: Miramax Home
Entertainment (with ICAIC).

Harrison, Faye. 1995. "The Persistent Power of 'Race' in the Cultural and
Political Economy of Racism." *Annual Review of Anthropology* 24: 47–74.

Hartigan, John Jr. 1999. *Racial Situations: Class Predicaments of Whiteness in
Detroit*. Princeton, NJ: Princeton University Press.

Helg, Aline. 1995. *Our Rightful Share: The Afro-Cuban Struggle for Equality,
1886–1912*. Chapel Hill: University of North Carolina Press.

Hernández-Reguant, Ariana. 2002. *Radio Taino and the Globalization of the
Cuban Culture Industries*. PhD diss., University of Chicago.

Heuman, Gad. 1981. *Between Black and White: Race, Politics, and the Free
Coloreds in Jamaica, 1792–1865*. Westport, CT: Greenwood Press.

Hodge, Derrick. 2001. "Colonization of the Cuban Body: The Growth of Male
Sex Work in Havana." *NACLA: Report on the Americas* 34 (5): 20–28.

Hoetink, Harry H. 1985. "'Race' and Color in the Caribbean." In *Caribbean
Contours*, edited by Sidney W. Mintz and Sally Price, 55–84. Baltimore, MD:
Johns Hopkins University Press.

Holt, Thomas C. 2000. *The Problem of Race in the Twenty-first Century*.
Cambridge, MA: Harvard University Press.

Humphrey, Caroline. 1999. "Traders, 'Disorder,' and Citizenship Regimes in
Provincial Russia." In *Uncertain Transition: Ethnographies of Change in
the Postsocialist World*, edited by Michael Burawoy and Katherine Verdery,
19–52. New York: Rowman & Littlefield.

Huntington, Samuel P. 1996. *The Clash of Civilizations and the Remaking of
World Order*. New York: Simon & Schuster.

Jackson, John L., Jr. 2001. *Harlemworld: Doing Race and Class in Contemporary
Black America*. Chicago: University of Chicago Press.

Jatar-Hausmann, Ana Julia. 1999. *The Cuban Way: Capitalism, Communism and
Confrontation*. W. Hartford, CT: Kumarian Press.

Johnston, Lynda. 2001. "(Other) Bodies and Tourism Studies." *Annals of Tourism
Research* 28 (January): 180–201.

Kempadoo, Kamala, ed. 1999. *Sun, Sex, and Gold: Tourism and Sex Work in the
Caribbean*. Lanham, MD: Rowman & Littlefield.

———. 2001. "Women of Color and the Global Sex Trade: Transnational Feminist
Perspectives." *Meridians: Feminisms, Race, Transnationalism* 1 (2): 28–51.

Knight, Franklin W. 2005. *Contemporary Caribbean Cultures and Societies in a
Global Context*. Chapel Hill: University of North Carolina Press.

Kutzinski, Vera M. 1993. *Sugar's Secrets: Race and the Erotics of Cuban
Nationalism*. Charlottesville: University Press of Virginia.

Latin American Network Information Center (LANIC). 2009. *Castro Speech Database.* Electronic document, http://lanic.utexas.edu/la/cb/cuba/castro. html (accessed September 4, 2009).

Lewis, K. Gordon . 1985. "The Contemporary Caribbean: A General Overview." In *Caribbean Contours,* edited by Sidney W. Mintz and Sally Price, 219–250. Baltimore, MD: Johns Hopkins University Press.

Lewellen, Ted C. 2002. *The Anthropology of Globalization: Cultural Anthropology Enters the 21st Century.* Westport, CT: Greenwood Publishing Group.

MacCannell, Dean. 1976. *The Tourist: A New Theory of the Leisure Class.* New York: Schocken.

Malinowski, Bronislaw. 1922. *Argonauts of the Western Pacific: An Account of Native Enterprise and Adventure in the Archipelagoes.* New York: E. P. Dutton & Co.

Martí, José. 1977. "Our America." In *Our America: Writings on Latin America and the Struggle for Cuban Independence,* edited by Philip S. Foner, 84–94. New York: Monthly Review Press.

Martinez-Alier, Vera. 1974. *Marriage, Class and Colour in Nineteenth-Century Cuba: A Study of Racial Attitudes and Sexual Values.* New York: Cambridge University Press.

McGarrity, Gayle, and Osvaldo Cárdenas. 1995. "Cuba." In *No Longer Invisible: Afro-Latin Americans Today,* edited by Minority Rights Group, 77–108. London: Minority Rights Publications.

Mintz, Sidney W. 1989. *Caribbean Transformations.* New York: Columbia University Press.

Montagu, M. F. Ashley. 1942. *Man's Most Dangerous Myth: The Fallacy of Race.* New York: Columbia University Press.

Moore, Carlos. 1988. *Castro, the Blacks, and Africa.* Los Angeles: Center for Afro-American Studies, University of California.

——— 2008. *Pichón: Race and Revolution in Castro's Cuba: A Memoir.* Chicago: Lawrence Hill Books.

Moore, Robin. 1997. *Nationalizing Blackness: Afrocubanismo and Artistic Revolution in Havana, 1920–1940.* Pittsburgh: University of Pittsburgh Press.

Murphy, Joseph M. 2001. "Yéyé Cachita: Ochún in a Cuban Mirror." In *Osun Across the Waters: A Yoruba Goddess in Africa and the Americas,* edited by Joseph M. Murphy and Mei-Mei Sanford, 87–100. Bloomington: University of Indiana Press.

Oficina Nacional Estadísticas. 2008. "Visitantes por Paises [Visitors by Country of Origin]," *Anuario Estadístico de Cuba.* Tourism Statistics, Table 15.3. Electronic document, http://www.one.cu/aec2008/esp/15_tabla_cuadro.htm (accessed September 6, 2009).

Ohmae, Kenichi. 1995. *The End of the Nation State: The Rise of Regional Economies.* New York: Free Press.

Omi, Michael, and Howard Winant. 1986. *Racial Formation in the United States: From the 1960s to the 1980s.* New York: Routledge & Kegan Paul.

Ortíz, Fernando. 1906. *Hampa afro-cubana: los negros brujos: apuntes para un estudio de etnología criminal* [*The Afro-Cuban Underworld. Black Witches. Notes for an Ethnology of Criminal Studies*]. Madrid, Librería de F. Fé.

———. 1986. *Los negros curros* [*The Black Dogs*]. La Habana: Editorial de Ciencias Sociales.

Pérez, Louis A., Jr. 1988. *Cuba: Between Reform and Revolution*. New York: Oxford University Press.

———. 1999. *On Becoming Cuban: Identity, Nationality and Culture*. Chapel Hill: University of North Carolina Press.

Pérez, Louis A., Jr., and Lars Schoultz. 2003. "Cuba/U.S. relations." Public talk, Community Church of Chapel Hill, North Carolina. March 31.

Pérez-Stable, Marifeli. 1993. *The Cuban Revolution: Origins, Course, and Legacy*. New York: Oxford University Press.

Pertierra, Anna Cristina. 2007. *Anthropology Matters Journal* 9 (1). Electronic journal, http://www.anthropologymatters.com/journal/2007–1/pertierra_2007_anthropology.htm (accessed September 5, 2009).

Rabinow, Paul. 1977. *Reflections on Fieldwork in Morocco*. Berkeley: University of California Press.

Ramírez, Rafael L. 1999. *What It Means to Be a Man: Reflections on Puerto Rican Masculinity*. Translated by Rosa E. Casper. New Brunswick, NJ: Rutgers University Press.

Reed, Susan. 1998. "The Politics and Poetics of Dance." *Annual Review of Anthropology* 27: 503–532.

"Remember the Maine." 1996. *Sea Tales*, VHS series. History Channel/A & E Home Video. New York: New Video Group.

Roland, L. Kaifa. 2004. "El Color No Importa: Tourism and Race in Contemporary Cuba." PhD diss., Duke University.

———. 2006. "Tourism and the *Negrificación* of Cuban Identity." *Transforming Anthropology*. 14(2): 151–162.

Rolando, Gloria, dir. 2001. "*Raíces de mi Corazon* [Roots of My Heart]." Film. Havana: Imagines del Caribe (independent filmmakers).

Rosendahl, Mona. 1997. *Inside the Revolution: Everyday Life in Socialist Cuba*. Ithaca, NY: Cornell University Press.

Ruíz, Ramón Eduardo. 1968. *Cuba: The Making of a Revolution*. New York: Norton.

Sawyer, Mark Q. 2006. *Racial Politics in Post-Revolutionary Cuba*. New York: Cambridge University Press.

Schwartz, Rosalie. 1997. *Pleasure Island: Tourism and Temptation in Cuba*. Lincoln: University of Nebraska Press.

Serra, Ana. 2007. *The "New Man" in Cuba: Culture and Identity in the Revolution*. Gainesville: University Press of Florida.

Sheller, Mimi. 2003. *Consuming the Caribbean: From Arawaks to Zombies*. New York: Routledge.

Simmons, Kimberly Eison. 2001. "A Passion for Sameness: Encountering a Black Feminist Self in Fieldwork in the Dominican Republic." In *Black Feminist*

Anthropology: Theory, Praxis, Politics and Poetics, edited by Irma McClaurin, 77–101. New Brunswick, NJ: Rutgers University Press.

Smith, Robert Freeman, ed. 1979. *Background to Revolution: The Development of Modern Cuba*. Huntington, NY: Robert Kiefer.

Smith, Valene L., and Maryann Brent. 2001. *Hosts and Guests Revisited: Tourism Issues of the 21st Century*. New York: Cognizant Communication Corp.

Sørensen, Ninna Nyberg. 1997. "There Are No Indians in the Dominican Republic: The Cultural Construction of Dominican Identities." In *Siting Culture: The Shifting Anthropological Object*, edited by Karen Fog Olwig and Kirsten Hastrup, 292–310. New York: Routledge.

Stanley, David. 2001. *Cuba*. Oakland, CA: Lonely Planet.

Stocking, George. 1994. "The Turn-of-the-Century Concept of Race." *Modernism/Modernity* 1 (1): 4–16.

Stoler, Ann Laura. 1995. *Race and the Education of Desire: Foucault's History of Sexuality and the Colonial Order of Things*. Durham, NC: Duke University Press.

Stoner, K. Lynne. 1991. *From the House to the Streets: the Cuban Woman's Movement for Legal Reform, 1898–1940*. Durham: Duke University Press.

Taylor, Frank F. 1993. *To Hell with Paradise: A History of the Jamaican Tourist Industry*. Pittsburgh: University of Pittsburgh Press.

Thomas, Deborah A. 2002. "Democratizing Dance: Institutional Transformation and Hegemonic Re-Ordering in Postcolonial Jamaica." *Cultural Anthropology* 17 (4): 512–550.

———. 2004. *Modern Blackness: Nationalism, Globalization, and the Politics of Culture in Jamaica*. Durham, NC: Duke University Press.

Trouillot, Michel-Rolph. 1991. "Anthropology and the Savage Slot: The Poetics and Politics of Otherness." In *Recapturing Anthropology: Working in the Present*, edited by Richard G. Fox, 17–44. Santa Fe, NM: School of American Research Press.

Twine, France Winddance. 1998. *Racism in a Racial Democracy: The Maintenance of White Supremacy in Brazil*. New Brunswick, NJ: Rutgers University Press.

Ulysse, Gina. 2007. *Downtown Ladies: Informal Commercial Importers, a Haitian Anthropologist, and Self-Making in Jamaica*. Chicago: University of Chicago Press.

Verdery, Katherine. 1996. *What Was Socialism and What Comes Next?* Princeton, NJ: Princeton University Press.

Wade, Peter. 1993. *Blackness and Race Mixture: The Dynamics of Racial Identity in Colombia*. Baltimore, MD: Johns Hopkins University Press.

Wallace, Michele. 1979. *Black Macho and the Myth of the Superwoman*. New York: Dial Press.

Whittle, Kate. 1997. "Tourism in Cuba." *Cuba Sí*. Electronic document, http://www.poptel.org.uk/cuba-solidarity/CubaSi-January/Turism.html (accessed March 2, 2000).

Woodruff, David. 1999. "Barter of the Bankrupt: The Demonetization in Russia's Federal State." In *Uncertain Transition: Ethnographies of Change in the Postsocialist World*, edited by Michael Burawoy and Katherine Verdery, 00–124. New York. Rowman & Littlefield.

Wright, Winthrop R. 1990. *Café Con Leche: Race, Class, and National Image in Venezuela*. Austin: University of Texas Press.

Yelvington, Kevin A. 2001. "The Anthropology of Afro-Latin America and the Caribbean: Diasporic Dimensions." *Annual Review of Anthropology* 30: 227–260.

Young, Robert. 1995. *Colonial Desire: Hybridity in Theory, Culture, and Race*. New York: Routledge.

INDEX

racism in, 4, 13, 65, 82
research in, 15
romance in, 17
security guards in, 2
Nivel de cultura, 36
Nonwhite *yumas,* 65–66

Obama, Barack, 92, 101
Orthodox party, 31
Ortíz, Fernando, 39

Pardos (coloreds), 7, 23, 29
Partido Independiente de Color
    (Independent Colored Party/PIC),
    28–29
"Passing," in race, 7
Pastors for Peace, 58
People of color. *See Pardos*
Pepe/pepa. *See Yuma*
Perestroika policy, 11, 13
Performance behavior, 8, 19, 29
Performativity, 65
Peso-dollar dual economy, 3, 92–93
Pesos convertibles (CUC), 45
Pieza (piece), 99
Pinar del Rio, Cuba, 15
Pingueros. See Sex tourism/industry
Pipo, 4–5, 6, 97, 98, 100
Platt Amendment, 28, 31
Playa embassy district, 15, 76, 78
Police harassment, 2, 20, 28, 54, 70, 74
Por la izquierda, 50–52
Prerevolution, 41–42, 88–89
Privilege
    place and, 67–75
    of tourists, 65
    of upper class, 23
    of whites, 4, 7
    of *yumas,* 78
Pro-socialist globalization, 13–15
Professional-class status, 58, 82, 97
Prostitutes/prostitution (*putas*), 1–2, 56,
    64, 71–75, 99. *See also* Sex tourism/
    industry

Race. *See also* Blackness; Mulato/mulata;
    Negro/negra; Whiteness; Whitening
anthropology and, 5–6
brownness, 23, 84
Caribbean and, 6–7, 23, 35–36, 98
constructions of, 6–8, 22–31, 35–36
Creole population, 24, 25
darkening and, 22, 40, 82
gendered, 37–41

jineteras and, 54–56
masculinity and, 39
meaning of, 4–8
mestizo, 2, 22, 23, 33, 75
"passing" in, 7
revolution and, 31–32
Racial democracy, 1, 2, 6, 22, 30, 35, 37
Racism
blackness and, 60, 84
Cuban revolution and, 32
against Cubans, 1–2, 66, 76,
    90, 100
Jim Crow laws and, 6, 28
marriage and, 60
against negros, 4–5
segregation and, 64, 90–91
whitening and, 2–3, 7, 22
Rastafarians, 36, 97, 98
Rationing/ration books (*libreta*), 21, 45, 48
Reflexivity in research, 17–18
Republican era, 24, 31
Research. *See* Methodology of research
Respectability, 39
Revolution. *See* Cuban revolution
Romantic relationships, 17–19, 60–61, 72, 74
Rosendahl, Mona, 45, 88
Rubios (blondes), 66
Rumba dance, 30

Santería religion, 30, 37, 59
Santiago-de-Cuba, 8, 15, 31, 67
Security guard employees, 75–76
Segregation, 64, 90–91
Service industry, 9
Sex tourism/industry, 71–75, 81–82. *See also*
    Prostitutes/prostitution
Sexuality, 6, 22, 37–39, 41–42, 55, 75, 81
Slavery
    abolition of, 25, 26
    blackness and, 23–24
    colonialism and, 9, 27, 28
    indentureship and, 22
Social Darwinism, 5–6, 62
Socialism (socialist system)
    capitalism *vs.,* 11–13, 89–91
    of Castro, Fidel, 87–88
    communism and, 11–13, 47
    economic organization and, 65
    Marxism (Marxist-Leninism), 12, 62, 81
    pro-socialist globalization, 13–15
    revolutionary ideal and, 11–13, 30, 87–89
    during Special Period, 65, 92–93
    tourism and, 2, 92
South American mainland, 14

CPSIA information can be obtained at www.ICGtesting.com
Printed in the USA
BVOW011635030712

294308BV00006B/3/P